ADVANCING ON II
with the
SQUARE IN A SQUARE® TECHNIQUE

In 1996 the original ADVANCING ON was published
with 36 pages, 12 quilts, 15 options, and no charts.
This is the revised edition of ADVANCING ON, BOOK 2.

By Jodi Barrows

PUBLISHING

1613 Lost Lake Drive • Keller, Texas 76248

TOLL FREE 1-888-624-6260   FAX 817-605-7420

EMAIL qyjodi@yahoo.com

WEB www.squareinasquare.com

ADVANCING ON II
with the
SQUARE IN A SQUARE® TECHNIQUE

REVISED 2004

By Jodi Barrows

CREDITS:

Once again a huge thank you and hug for those who help me day in and day out! All of my staff are so special and talented. I could not accomplish all of this without these wonderful people:

Kasi Skelly, Quilt Support

Amber Arnold, Literary Support

JaLonn Carter-Stanley, Machine Quilting

Last but not least, my certified teachers for proofing, Kay Roberts, Rosie de Leon-McCrady, Barbara Handler, Bonnie Taylor

Photography: J. Royce Reid

Graphic Design: Laurie Frasier, Grand Junction, CO

Printing: Branch Smith Printing, Fort Worth, TX

ISBN 0-9716961-7-9

6th Printing

Are you on our mailing list to receive our newsletter by email?

If not, please call or email:

1-888-624-6260 • qyjodi@yahoo.com

CONTENTS

INTRODUCTION

In 1996 the original "Advancing On" book was published by Quiltingly Yours, Inc. This was the second book using the Square in a Square® technique. Advancing On was written to give more information on this revolutionary strip piecing system. Eight new options, for a total of 15 different triangle units were now available for the Square in a Square® system. The incredible fact of never cutting or sewing a triangle unit was amazing. I was having fun teaching others and they were having a wonderful time making wonderful quilts. I was teaching them how to have speed and accuracy, quality as well as quantity of quilt tops. We were all having fun and it was incredible! Turning squares and strips into triangle units was remarkable!

The orginal "Advancing On" went to print 7 times. The book consisted of 36 pages, 12 quilts, 15 options and no charts. The book was meant to be the main core workbook of the technique system. The system grew so fast that the book became out dated as the main workbook. Even though the name is similar, "Advancing On II" is a whole new book with 88 pages, 27 charts, 15 quilts, over 60 block sizes and 17 options.

If you are looking for a way to produce quality quilt tops with speed and accuracy, then look no more! Wecome to the Square in a Square® way!

Let's talk a little about constructing a quilt. I would like to tell you some hints about getting started and what works well for me. I never cut the whole quilt top out at the same time. I'm always anxious to get the fabric selection together. I can't wait to see the interaction and contrast of the fabric. If I like the way it is working together then I cut and sew a little more. I like to be able to move the color of fabric around if I need to. If all of the quilt is cut, I can't do that, and then what? I'm boxed in a corner with my yardage cut up. Next, I want to make sure I understand the cutting directions. Cutting a few at a time gives me room to make changes and alterations if necessary.

Last, when I'm finished with the quilt, satisfied, that's when I'm done. What I mean is that the quilt can be any size you want. Maybe I had good intentions to make a queen size quilt, but it didn't keep me interested, so I just go ahead and decide that I'm finished. The quilt is complete as the size that I have decided. If I had cut the whole quilt, I would have wasted fabric on an unfinished queen size quilt. That is wasted fabric. We all know that we are not getting back to that project to complete it. Get my point? This is suppose to make us feel good and be fun. Finishing a wonderful quilt is so exciting and fun. You decide as you go what you want.

TIPS:

• The Magic Math is only needed when you create a design from scratch.

• Remember to sew a "scant" 1/4" seam.

• Spray starch helps to keep washed fabric from moving.

• A finger space between the square on the strip is all that's needed, when sewing the basic square.

• Blunt corners are good.

• Use short strips on side 3 and side 4 when sewing the basic square.

• If your option is too large or small, check:
  1. center square size
  2. seam allowance
  3. the way you lay your ruler on the sewn square.

As always I consider my books to be workbooks. I want to give you lots of information to help you be creative.

I don't prewash my fabric. I find piecing is more accurate with the sizing in the fabric. If I'm concerned about it running, I test it and treat as necessary. I also like the sunscreen left in it during storage. It keeps the fabric fresh until I'm ready to use it. I also like the cotton bat and cotton fabric to shrink together after the quilt is finished. It gives it the antique look and feel I love so much!

What do I do with the fabric trimmed off the basic square? Use that funny triangle piece to sew to the side of a smaller center square, as long as the triangle scrap is large enough to get a good trim on your new Square in a Square® option. That's how a lot of my smaller or miniature quilts are made. It doesn't have to be a strip sewn to the side of your square. It could be that waste triangle unit, from a previous option cutting.

Why do you tell us to trim up to the point of the center square on some of the options and to trim leaving 1/4" off of the tip of the center square on the other options? This moves the seam allowances so that when you cut the option apart, the points of the triangles won't be lost in your next seam. The different options move the seam allowances with the trimming of the basic square.

Use a stiletto at the junctions of your seams to hold your squares where you want. It works better than a pin. When a pin is pushed down and back through the fabric where multi-seams are located it can move the exact point of your triangle points and cause your piece to be off when you open to press. A stiletto can keep seam allowance flaps in place and keep points sharper. Remember that the right tool for the job gives us better work and makes the job easier.

When cutting strip size it may be easier to cut 1/4ths than 1/8ths. You can round the strip size up to the nearest 1/4th. The excess will be trimmed off.

What is Magic Math™? Each option or triangle unit has its own Magic Math™. The Magic Math™ is used when you are adapting a pattern to this method of strip piecing. The point of each Magic Math™ equation is to find the cut size of the center square.

You may notice I recommend a 1/4th inch foot for the machine. When a student uses a mark on the machine itself, it gets in the way or it can't be seen with this technique.

What about the bias edge? This is one of the most frequently asked questions. When you are sewing your strips and squares in the basic step of getting started and the pressing of your seams, out...You are working with straight of grain which is good. This will keep your unit in control. All of the cutting, sewing, pressing, progress work is in the straight of grain. This is one of the steps that keeps your work flat and points sharp. When you trim your square to whichever option you are making, you then get a bias edge. At that point you will continue to sew onto your block or use it as a block, and usually to the straight of grain in the connecting. All of the steps that normally stretch your work are completed in the basic steps with straight of grain. Spray starch helps your fabric keep its size. Or use unwashed, tested fabric with the sizing still in it. Harriet Hargrave's book talks about dye testing and not washing fabric. I highly recommend her book on Textiles & Machine quilting. If you are having trouble with a bias edge, place it on the bottom next to the feed dogs. This will help feed it into the machine when sewing two units together.

GENERAL DIRECTIONS

Rotary Equipment

All the quilts were cut using rotary cutting tools. Always have a sharp blade in your cutter and a nice size mat. Serious quilters should consider having several sizes of self healing mats. Large pieces of fabric need a large mat; scraps can be cut on a smaller mat.

Use an accurate rotary ruler with clear measurements, including 1/8" marks. You will need a Square in a Square® (SnS) ruler or a ruler with 30°, 45°, and 60° lines. The SnS ruler was developed specifically for these quilts and makes cutting angles a breeze. See inside back cover for ordering.

Sewing Machine

Use a clean, oiled sewing machine with a size 70 or 80 needle. Make sure the tension is adjusted to produce a smooth seam.

Iron

A heavy, hot, steam iron will improve the quality of your work. Keep it close to your machine, for frequent pressing is a basic. A good rule to remember is to press to the dark or to the largest area without seams.

Fabric

Use 100% cotton, quality fabric. Yardage given is actual, plus 10% for shrinkage and small cutting errors.

I don't prewash fabric, repeat, I don't prewash. I find piecing is more accurate with sizing in the fabric. If I'm concerned about it running, I test it and treat as necessary.

Batting

There are many choices in batting. I have used most of them and like cotton/poly the best. It gives the quilts an antique look. Pretreat the batting as suggested on the package.

Borders

To find the correct border length, measure the center of the quilt from raw edge to raw edge. Cut two side borders this length and sew on. Repeat for the width, measurement includes the side borders. Measuring along the outside edges can cause the border to ripple. You may have to ease the border to fit. If so, put the fullness on the bottom, against the feed dogs.

Finishing

Cut the batting and backing 4" longer and wider than the quilt top. Layer all together and baste. Use large hand stitches if hand quilting and 1" safety pins if machine quilting.

Quilting is fun and time consuming. However, it can add a lot of character to the quilt. Heavy quilting is always admired. Plan your quilting to enhance the quilt. Make hand stitches even and as small as you can.

Machine quilting techniques have improved greatly. A walking foot is a must for straight line quilting and binding. A darning foot and dropping the feed dogs will allow you to free motion most any design. It is a lot of fun, so keep trying. Small and medium quilts are the easiest to maneuver on the sewing machine. Use cotton thread in the bobbin. Try nylon .004 in the top of the machine and adjust the top tension. For best results, use a backing fabric with a design.

Fabric Dye

For an older muted look, over dye the quilt. Dilute one box of ecru or tan color dye in a cup of warm/hot water. Add it to a full washer of warm water. Mix or agitate it for a moment or two on delicate or short cycle, cool rinse. Add your quilt, walk away and don't worry! Ha! I stand right by my washer. Stretch it out to dry. In the daily Kansas 20 MPH wind, it only takes about 20 minutes to dry. I put a sheet over the hammock and lay the quilt on that. Don't let it fade by forgetting it out in the sun, or let a bird fly over. I need a sitter, so our 15 lb. cat, Samson, lies in the middle for a cool nap and the birds stay away.

Cutting

You will be cutting strips of fabric from yardage or fat quarters. Cutting instructions are given for full widths, 42" - 44". If using fat quarters, simply cut twice as many strips as stated. Fold or layer the fabric. Make a clean up cut on one

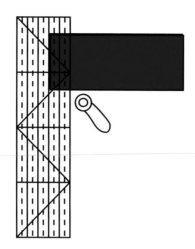

edge. You can cut about six layers at once. More than that is risky, as the fabric shifts.

Often the directions call for crosscuts. These are made of strips or strip sets (strips sewn together).

Machine Piecing

Machine piecing is strong, fast and accurate. Learn to sew a 1/4" seam; it is a must. To test your 1/4" seam, stitch together three 1-1/2" x 6" strips along the 6" edge. Press. The unit will measure 3-1/2" x 6" if the seam allowance is accurate. If it doesn't, practice until it does.

For more accurate piecing, try using spray starch on the fabric before sewing. This is very helpful with miniatures or with pre washed fabric.

3-1/2"

When you have two pieces that should fit together, but don't, you will have to ease them. Pin them well and make them fit so seams and points will match up. The fullest piece should feed through the machine on the bottom. The feed dogs will help ease the fullness more evenly and the foot on top will slightly stretch the top layer.

Chain Piecing

Chain piecing has always been a natural for me. I did it before I knew someone else had invented it! Keep sewing the units, one after the other, into the machine without lifting the presser foot or cutting threads. When you change to another part of the pattern, or you have about a mile of pieces on the back of your machine, stop and cut them apart, or have the kids help to snip them. I also use a runner, which is a small scrap of fabric. I run it into the machine when I don't have a pattern piece to sew or I need to stop on the chain piecing. It just leaves the machine in neutral, ready to sew. With a runner and chain piecing, you don't have a mess with clipping all of those loose threads, or lift the presser foot.

Square in a Square®

All of the quilts in this book are based on my Square in a Square® (SnS) piecing technique. This method creates squares within each other by sewing strips and squares together. It results in extra clean cuts and accuracy not found with other methods. There are several options to the technique, you will be amazed at how versatile the SnS technique can be.

Basic Steps for Square in a Square®

All of the quilts included give detailed cutting instructions. If you want to design your own quilt, the directions which follow give formulas for calculating measurements. Round to the nearest 1/8". Use the chart below to convert the decimals on the calculator to fractions.

1/8 = .125	5/8 = .625
1/4 = .25	3/4 = .75
3/8 = .375	7/8 = .875
1/2 = .5	

Since there is rounding involved in this technique the following will help you to be more accurate.

When sewing a bias and straight grain edge together, always ease or stretch the bias piece to fit the straight grain piece. Also, whenever possible, sew with straight grain edges on top and bias on the bottom.

You will be making a "Square in a Square®". This is sewing strips and squares together to create squares within each other. When you sew first and then cut the triangles, it allows extra clean cuts, and accurate blocks or units for blocks. No triangle stretch or bias worry. You may cut straight or bias fabric strips. You will be amazed at how versatile this "Square in a Square®" technique can be! Let's get started.

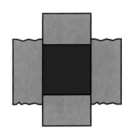

- Lay the corner strip face up on your sewing machine. Place the square face down on the strip with edges even. Sew 1/4" along edge of square. Lay the next square down on the strip and continue on in the chain piecing method.

- Repeat for the opposite side of the square.

- Cut the squares apart and press open – seams out.

- Sew strips to the other two sides of the square

  Hint: to save fabric, just sew a strip the length of center square plus 1/2"

- Press open – seams out.

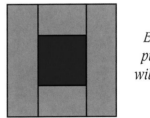

Either picture will work

- Cut a "Square in a Square®" block. The "Square in a Square®" ruler makes this step easy. Match the corner on the inside square with the corresponding angle on the ruler. Trim all four corners according to the option you choose. Notice that sometimes the corners are blunted just a little. This won't affect the finished square at all. You now have a "Square in a Square®".

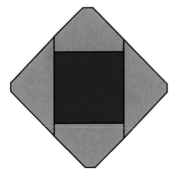
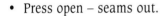

⦿PTION 1

When cutting your "SnS®", leave 1/4" seam allowance on all 4 sides of your square, don't sew or cut off the tip of the inside squares.

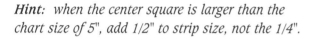

Use this math formula to find your strip size:

To find the strip size for the corner, measure center square..... Divide in half....Add 1/4"...... Cut strip this measurement for the next row to sew around your square.

Hint: when the center square is larger than the chart size of 5", add 1/2" to strip size, not the 1/4".

Hint: to save fabric, just sew a strip the length of the center square plus 1/2".

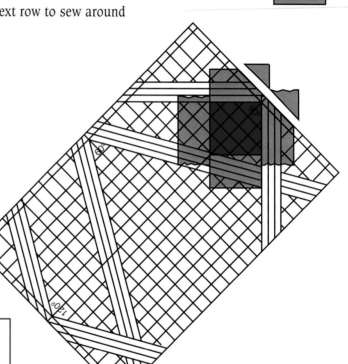

Chart for Option #1
Total Finished Size

Sewn-Finished or Graph Paper Size	Cut Center Square	Cut Strip Size
1	1-1/4	3/4
1-1/4	1-3/8	1
1-1/2	1-5/8	1-1/8
1-3/4	1-3/4	1-1/4
2	2	1-1/4
2-1/4	2-1/8	1-3/8
2-1/2	2-1/4	1-3/8
2-3/4	2-1/2	1-1/2
3	2-5/8	1-5/8
3-1/4	2-3/4	1-5/8
3-1/2	3	1-3/4
3-3/4	3-1/8	1-7/8
4	3-3/8	1-7/8
4-1/4	3-1/2	2
4-1/2	3-5/8	2-1/8
4-3/4	3-7/8	2-1/4
5	4	2-1/4

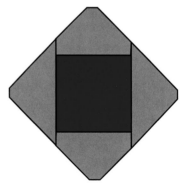

Hint: when cutting strip size it may be easier to cut 1/4ths than 1/8ths. You can round the strip size up to the nearest 1/4th.

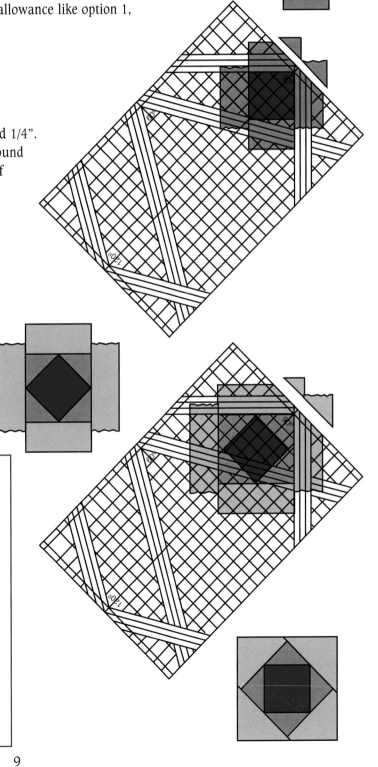

You may continue to add strips to enlarge your "SnS®".

Refer to the math formula to find the width for cutting your strips. The cut square (like option 1) is the "SnS®" you are adding on to.

• Remember each time you trim up to leave 1/4" seam allowance like option 1, when cutting new "SnS®".

"SnS®" Math Formula

Use this math formula to find your strip size:

Measure your new outside square. Divide in half..... add 1/4". Cut strip that measurement for the next row to sew around the square. For 120° and 60° angles, measure width of diamond and do the same math formula.

Hint: remember sewn-finished or graph paper size are all the same size. Cut or raw edge is the same.

Hint: when the center square starts to be 5" or 6" or bigger, add 1/2" to strip size: not the 1/4".

Chart for Option #2

Sewn-Finished or Graph Paper Size	Cut Center Square	Cut 1st Strip	Cut 2nd Strip
2	1-1/2	1	1-1/8
2-1/4	1-5/8	1	1-1/4
2-1/2	1-3/4	1-1/8	1-3/8
2-3/4	1-7/8	1-1/4	1-1/2
3	2	1-1/4	1-1/2
3-1/4	2-1/8	1-3/8	1-5/8
3-1/2	2-1/4	1-3/8	1-3/4
3-3/4	2-3/8	1-1/2	1-7/8
4	2-1/2	1-1/2	1-7/8
4-1/4	2-5/8	1-5/8	2
4-1/2	2-3/4	1-3/4	2-1/4
4-3/4	2-7/8	1-3/4	2-1/4
5	3	1-3/4	2-1/4

$\mathcal{O}$PTION **3** - FLYING GEESE

Cut your "SnS®" in half. You will need to leave 1/4" seam allowance at the top (north) and bottom (south) sides of your "SnS®" when you trim up the corners. Cut like "Option 1" on the north and south side of your "SnS®". On the opposite side of your square, trim up to the point of the inside square. Put the tip of the line in the tip of the center square. Cut in half as shown.

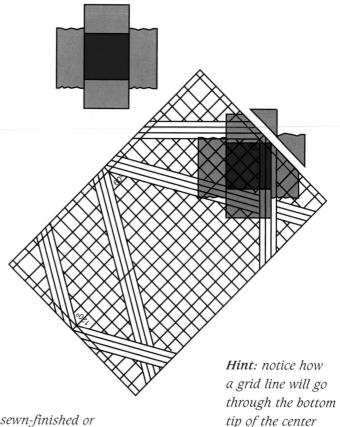

To make these so they will match up against an Option #1 or #2... add 3/8" to cut center square size, then use regular "Square in a Square®" formula to get corner strip size.

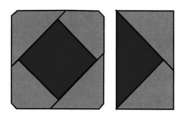

Magic Math™: Draw your pattern out on graph paper. Measure sewn center square and add 7/8" to the center square for cut size. Figure strip size as always.

Hint: remember sewn-finished or graph paper size is all the same measurement. Cut or raw edge is the same measurement.

Hint: notice how a grid line will go through the bottom tip of the center square. This will help keep the block square.

Chart for Option #3 Flying Geese

For Sewn Size of Rectangle Unit	Cut Center Square	Cut Strip Size
1 x 2	2-1/4	1-3/8
1-1/4 x 2-1/2	2-5/8	1-5/8
1-1/2 x 3	3	1-3/4
1-3/4 x 3-1/2	3-3/8	2
2 x 4	3-3/4	2-1/8
2-1/4 x 4-1/2	4	2-1/4
2-1/2 x 5	4-3/8	2-1/2
2-3/4 x 5-1/2	4-3/4	2-5/8
3 x 6	5-1/8	2-7/8

Hint: when using large Flying Geese this may be helpful. Before cutting your #3 in half, stay stitch 1/4" from the center cut lines on each side.

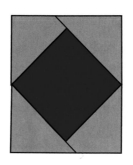

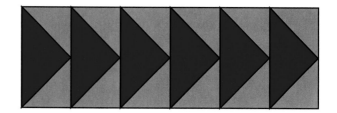

10

$\mathcal{O}$PTION **4** - HALF SQUARE TRIANGLES

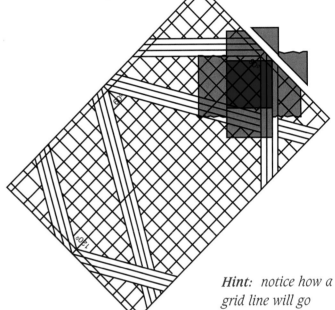

Cut all 4 sides up to the point. Cut in half again. It makes 4 squares with triangles! The "SnS®" squares can be cut to make half square triangles. There are two formulas for making the half square triangles. If you want half square triangles so that four of them sewn together make a unit the size of a "SnS®", **cut the center square 3/4" larger than** the center square of the full "SnS®". Cut the corner strips half the width of the center square. For example: The full square uses a cut square of 2-1/2" and corners strips 1-1/2" wide. The half square triangles are made with a 3-1/4" square (2-1/2" + 3/4") and corner strips of 1-5/8" (3-1/4" ÷ 2).

If you just want half square triangles and they don't have to match up with a full "SnS®", use the following formula. **Multiply the desired cut size of the half square triangle by 1.414 and add 1/2" to get the size of the center square.** Round to the nearest 1/8". The corner strips are half the width of the center square. For example: You want 3" half square triangles (finished size 2-1/2"). The center square is cut 4-3/4" or [(3" x 1.414) + 1/2"]. The corner strips are cut 2-3/8" (4-3/4" ÷ 2). Cut all four sides up to the point like the east west sides on Option #3. Next cut the square into quarters.

Hint: notice how a grid line will go through the bottom tip of the center square. This will help keep the block square.

To use the option charts you need to know the cut (raw) size or sewn size of the square unit.

 or

Then follow the measurements on the Option #4 chart.

Chart for Option #4
Half Square Triangles

For Sewn Size of 1/2 Square Triangle Unit	Cut Center Square	Cut Strip Size
1/2	2	1-1/4
1	2-5/8	1-1/2
1-1/4	3	1-3/4
1-1/2	3-3/8	2
1-3/4	3-5/8	2-1/8
2	4	2-1/4
2-1/4	4-3/8	2-1/2
2-1/2	4-3/4	2-5/8
2-3/4	5	2-3/4
3	5-1/2	3

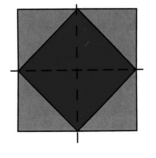

1/8 = .125	5/8 = .625
1/4 = .25	3/4 = .75
3/8 = .375	7/8 = .875
1/2 = .5	

$\mathscr{O}$PTION 5

Use any pattern in place of the solid middle square. Figure strip size as always.

When cutting your "SnS®", leave 1/4" seam allowance on all 4 sides of your square, don't sew or cut off the tip of the inside squares.

Use this math formula to find your strip size:

To find the strip size for the corner, measure center square..... Divide in half....Add 1/4"...... Cut strip this measurement for the next row to sew around your square.

Hint: to save fabric, just sew a strip the length of the center square plus 1/2".

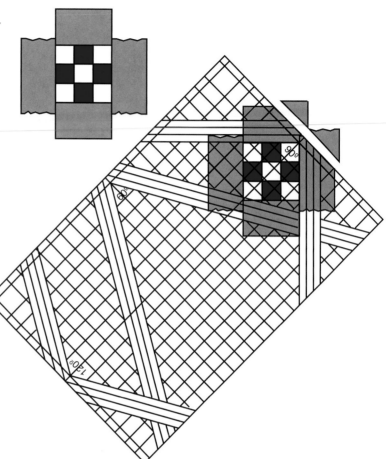

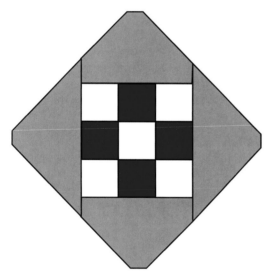

Refer to Option #1 for special tips.

Hint: when cutting strip size it may be easier to cut 1/4ths than 1/8ths. You can round the strip size up to the nearest 1/4th.

Hint: remember sewn-finished or graph paper size are all the same size. Cut or raw edge is the same.

Chart for Option #5
Total Finished Size

Finished Size	Cut Center Square	Cut Strip Size
1	1-1/4	3/4
1-1/4	1-3/8	1
1-1/2	1-5/8	1-1/8
1-3/4	1-3/4	1-1/4
2	2	1-1/4
2-1/4	2-1/8	1-3/8
2-1/2	2-1/4	1-3/8
2-3/4	2-1/2	1-1/2
3	2-5/8	1-5/8
3-1/4	2-3/4	1-5/8
3-1/2	3	1-3/4
3-3/4	3-1/8	1-7/8
4	3-3/8	1-7/8
4-1/4	3-1/2	2
4-1/2	3-5/8	2-1/8
4-3/4	3-7/8	2-1/4
5	4	2-1/4

$\mathcal{O}$PTION **6** - USE YOUR IMAGINATION

Put anything in the middle.

Put a strip on 1, 2, or 3 sides of the option. (Depends on what triangle unit you are designing.)

Each time you sew a strip on the side of your square you will get a triangle in that location.

Trim square leaving 1/4" seam off of tip or right up to the tip, depending on where you need your seam allowance to be.

Place ruler 90° on inside square tip to trim off bottom leaving 1/4".

Trim sides up to the tip using 1 line on the ruler. This trimming is like Option #3, Flying Geese. You will have a slight blunt on bottom two triangles.

Feel free to mix any of the options together to create your own unique units. Play around with this to see what you can make. Revert back to your basic center options to figure math and remember you can call if you need help.

Hint: *press all of your seams out on the center square. This will allow fabric in the seam allowance off of the tip of the center square.*

Hint: *mix any of the options to create new units.*

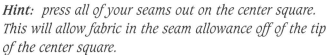

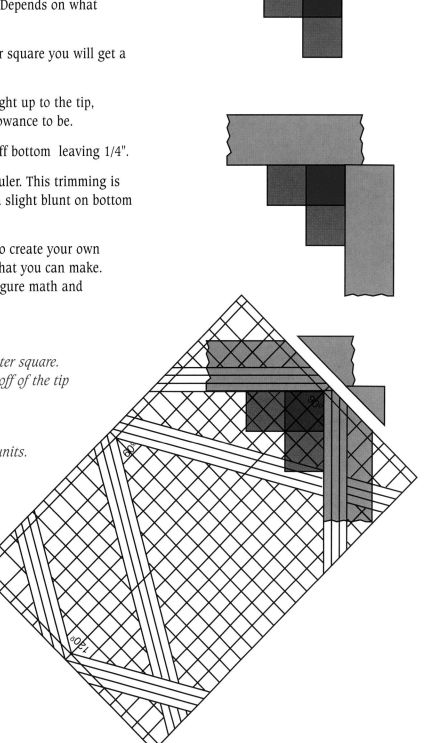

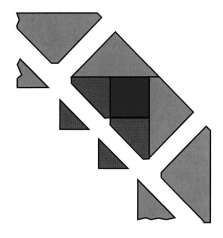

13

Substitute a 60° diamond for the center square. You will be working with rectangles and long thin triangles. Cut the diamonds from a strip of fabric. Lay the 60° angle on a ruler along the horizontal edge of the strip. Trim the strip along the edge of the ruler. Cut segments the same width as the strip. Check the angle every 3-4 cuts to make sure it is still 60°, recutting if necessary.

Add corner strips. Use the same formula for finding the width of the corner strips as used for squares (width of diamond strip ÷ 2 + 1/4"). Sew strips to the two opposite sides first. Trim even with the diamond.

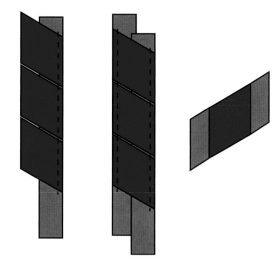

Sew corner strips to the remaining two sides.

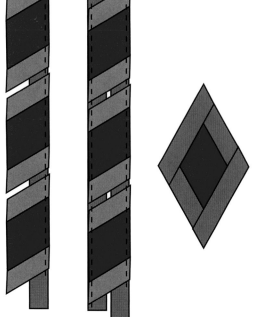

Hint: remember sewn-finished or graph paper size is all the same measurement. Cut or raw edge is the same measurement.

Hint: short strips may be sewn to sides 3 & 4. Refer to pg. 7 of basic square sewing.

You may make the Diamond "SnS®" like any of the Options listed here. Remember that Option #1 leaves 1/4" seam allowances on all four corners.

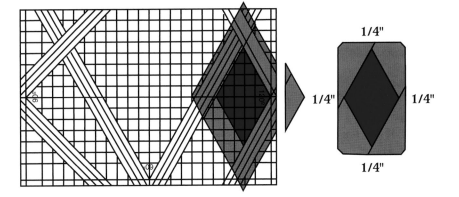

Cutting Option #3 is slightly different for a diamond than for a square center. Leave 1/4" at the sharp (60°) points of the diamond. Leave 1/8" at the other (120°) points. This is necessary to get good star points.

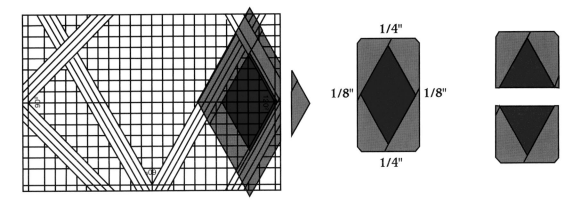

If using a "SnS®" Ruler, simply match the corner of the diamond to the angles on the ruler, leaving the seam allowance necessary.

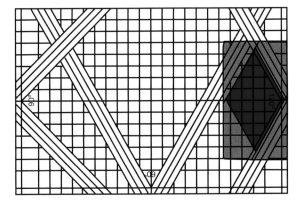

We have barely touched the tip of the diamond iceberg with everything that can be accomplished using the SnS® technique. Keep watching for more diamond information. Check our website and newsletter. The video is also a super way to visually see this technique.

Chart for Option #7

Sewn-Finished or Graph Paper Size Rectangle	Cut Strip for center Diamond	Cut Strip Size
1 x 1-3/4	1-3/8	1
1-1/4 x 2	1-1/2	1
1-1/2 x 2-1/2	1-3/4	1-1/8
1-3/4 x 3	2	1-1/4
2 x 3-1/2	2-1/4	1-3/8
2-1/4 x 4	2-1/2	1-1/2
2-1/2 x 4-1/4	2-3/4	1-5/8
2-3/4 x 4-5/8	2-7/8	1-3/4
3 x 5-1/4	3-1/4	1-7/8
3-1/4 x 5-3/4	3-3/8	2
3-1/2 x 6-1/4	3-1/2	2
3-3/4 x 6-5/8	3-3/4	2-1/8
4 x 7	4	2-1/4
4-1/4 x 7-1/2	4-1/4	2-3/8

*O*PTION **8**

Sew a "SnS®" block just like Option #1. Leave 1/4"
seam allowance off the tip of the inside square on all
4 corners. When cutting your block apart, cut across
from tip to opposite tip. Repeat for other side,
yielding 4 units.

Math for Option #8: Draw your pattern on graph
paper or know your sewn size of your corner square.
Double that size and add 1" for the cut center square
size of your "SnS®". Figure strip size as always.

Chart for Option #8

Sewn Corner Square Size	Cut Center Square	Strip Size
1	3	1-3/4
1-1/4	3-1/2	2
1-1/2	4	2-1/4
1-3/4	4-1/2	2-1/2
2	5	2-3/4
2-1/4	5-1/2	3
2-1/2	6	3-1/4
2-3/4	6-1/2	3-1/2
3	7	3-3/4

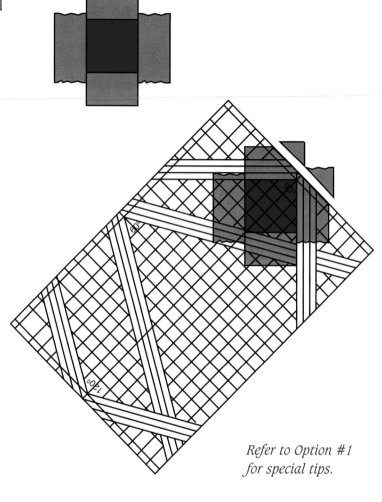

*Refer to Option #1
for special tips.*

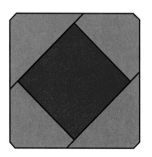

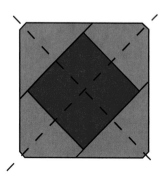

**CORNER
SQUARE**

16

Sew around your center square twice. Cut once corner to corner. For this option the block is trimmed differently. You will need to leave 1/4" seam allowance at the top and bottom sides of your "SnS®". On the opposite two sides of your square trim up to the point of the center inside square. This is like Option #3.

Continue another row of strips around your "SnS®". Trim like Option #1, leaving 1/4" off each tip. Two sides will look like you cut and sewed the tips off. This is correct, don't fret!

Cut in half, cutting across the open or flat tip corner.

Math for Option #9: Draw your pattern out on graph paper. Measure sewn center square and add 7/8" to the center square for cut size. Figure strip size as always.

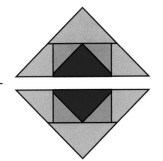

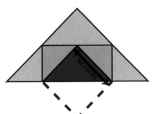

Hint: remember sewn-finished or graph paper size is all the same measurement. Cut or raw edge is the same measurement.

 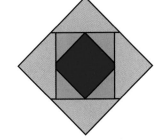 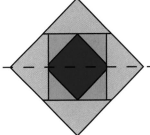

Units can be used to form a star.

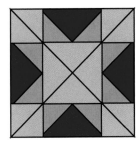

Chart for Option #9 - Flying Geese

For Sewn Size of inside rectangle flying goose	Cut Center Square	Cut Strip Size For First Row	Cut Strip Size For Second Row
1 x 2	2-1/4	1-3/8	1-3/4
1-1/4 x 2-1/2	2-5/8	1-5/8	2
1-1/2 x 3	3	1-3/4	2-1/4
1-3/4 x 3-1/2	3-3/8	2	2-1/2
2 x 4	3-3/4	2-1/8	2-3/4
2-1/4 x 4-1/2	4	2-1/4	3
2-1/2 x 5	4-3/8	2-1/2	3-1/4
2-3/4 x 5-1/2	4-3/4	2-5/8	3-1/2
3 x 6	5-1/8	2-7/8	4

Hint: when using large Flying Geese this may be helpful. Before cutting your #3 in half, stay stitch 1/4" from the center cut lines on each side.

Sew a "SnS®" block. Cut up to the point of the inside square. This is like Option #4. Use 1 line on the ruler (90°) and place it over the seam, right up to the point. Be careful not to trim off too much or too little.

Figure strip size as always and sew around your block again. Trim 2nd row leaving 1/4" off of tip, like Option #1. Your inside square will now be blunted.

Cut in half corner to corner both ways yielding 4 units. Make sure you have 1/4" seam allowance on inside blunt square.

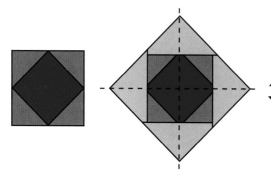

THIS CUT SIZE

To use the option charts you need to know the cut (raw) size or sewn size of the square unit.

 or

Then follow the measurements on the Option #10 chart.

Hint: *remember sewn-finished or graph paper size is all the same measurement. Cut or raw edge is the same measurement.*

Chart for Option #10

Cut Size of Square that will be 1/2 Square Triangles	Cut for Center Square	Cut for First Row	Cut for Second Row
1	2	1-1/4	1-1/2
1-1/2	2-5/8	1-1/2	2
1-3/4	3	1-3/4	2-1/4
2	3-3/8	2	2-1/2
2-1/4	3-5/8	2-1/8	3
2-1/2	4	2-1/4	3-1/4
2-3/4	4-3/8	2-1/2	3-1/2
3	4-3/4	2-5/8	3-5/8
3-1/4	5	2-3/4	3-3/4
3-1/2	5-1/2	3	4-1/4

Math for Option #10: Draw your pattern out on graph paper. Measure the sewn size of your half square triangle. Multiply the desired cut size of that square triangle unit by 1.414, and add 1/2" to get the square size for the center square of your "SnS®". Round to the nearest 1/8". Figure corner strips as always.

For example: You want 3" half square triangles (finished size 2-1/2"). The center square is cut 4-3/4" or [(3" x 1.414) + 1/2"]. The corner strips are cut 2-3/8" (4-3/4" ÷ 2). Cut all four sides up to the point like the east and west sides on Option #3.

1/8 = .125	
1/4 = .25	
3/8 = .375	
1/2 = .5	
5/8 = .625	
3/4 = .75	
7/8 = .875	

Sew a "SnS®" block. Like Option #2 we will sew around the block twice. The first time we trim we will leave 1/4" seam allowance off the tip. The second row will be trimmed right up to the tip: Refer to Option #4 up to the tip trimming and tips.

Cut the block in half twice yielding 4 units.

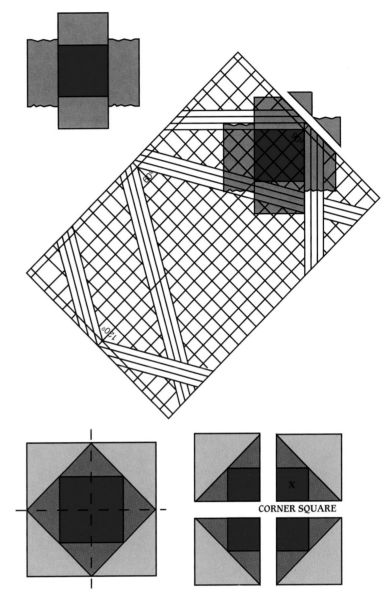

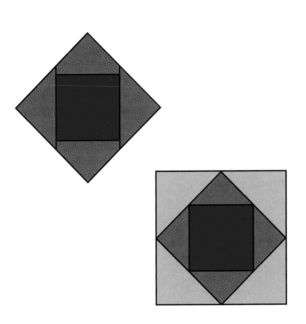

CORNER SQUARE

Chart for Option #11

Sewn Size of Corner Square	Cut for Center Square	Cut for First Row	Cut for Second Row
1	3	1-3/4	2-1/4
1-1/4	3-1/2	2	3
1-1/2	4	2-1/4	3-1/4
1-3/4	4-1/2	2-1/2	3-1/2
2	5	2-3/4	3-3/4
2-1/4	5-1/2	3	4-1/4
2-1/2	6	3-1/4	4-1/2
3	7	3-3/4	5-1/4

Math for Option #11: Draw your pattern on graph paper or know your sewn size of your corner square. Double that size and add 1" for the cut center square size of your "SnS®". Figure strip size as always.

Hint: remember sewn-finished or graph paper size is all the same measurement. Cut or raw edge is the same measurement.

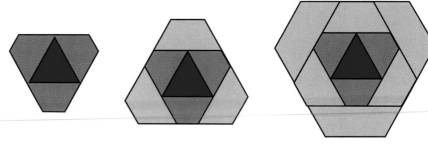

Sew a "SnS®" block. Use a triangle, square, or diamond for the center. Always trim leaving 1/4" seam allowance off of the tip. Keep sewing strips to your "SnS®". In the pineapple block the strip width always stays the same size. As you cut and sew your block, the shape will change. Don't get confused, each round has 4 sides, except the triangle. (It will grow to 6 sides.) Continue placing the corresponding angle of the ruler on the seam to trim it up.

Hint: after 2 or 4 rounds you will have 8 sides. Work with 4 at a time. At that point you will be squaring the unit up, no speical ruler placement.

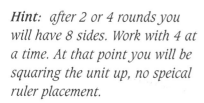

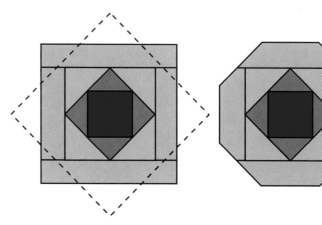

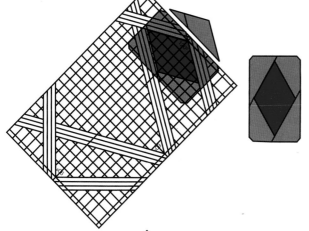

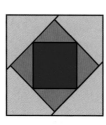

There is no math formula for this option. Use whatever center size you wish and strip width you like. The thinner the strip the slower the block grows. Normally the strip width is a little wider than the center.

Refer to Option #7 on pg. 14, and Pineapple Diamond, pg. 67, for diamond cutting.

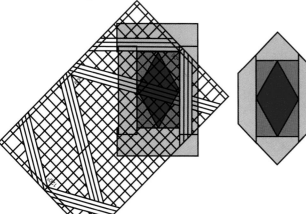

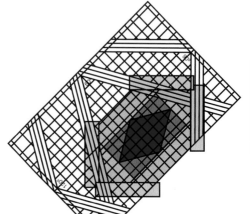

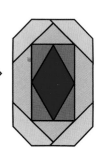

Triangle Strip Cutting for Option 12

Cut the strip the size you need, example 2". Lay the edge of the 60° line on the edge of your fabric strip. Make a clean up cut. Now flip your ruler with each cut creating an equilateral traingle. Use the edge or "tip" of the fabric to get the sizing. It takes a little practice, but not hard. Look at what you're making under the ruler, to make the correct cut.

Sew center unit (triangle-diamond-square) to the strip placing unit on top of the strip, just like the other options and sewing the basic square. Clip or separate.

Press unit open and cut two short strips to sew to sides 2 and 3. Trim with 60° in tip of triangle, leaving the 1/4" seam allowance on all 3 corners.

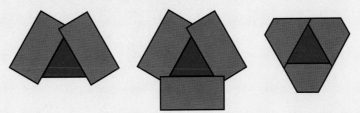

Each time a new row of strips are sewn around the center unit, the strips only have to cover the side. On the 2nd or 3rd time around the unit you will start to have 6 sides.

Place the 60° line at the edge of the SnS ruler at the tip or edge of the last inside row and the 60° line will cover the seam.

Continue to sew around the center unit with next row of strip. The next row will be sewn where the intersection of strips are. Repeat with each row of strips.

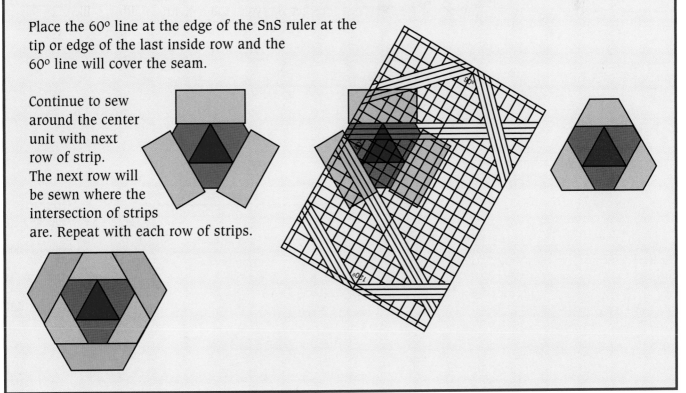

Sew a "SnS®" block. Sew around the block 3 times. Trim leaving 1/4" off of the tip of your square, on row 1 and 3. Trim up to the tip on the 2nd row.

Cut the block in half from corner to corner, twice, yielding 4 units.

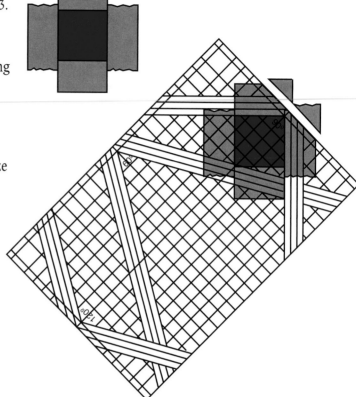

Math for Option #13: Draw your pattern out on graph paper or know your sewn size of your corner square. Double that size and add 1" for the cut center square size of your "SnS®". Figure strip size as always.

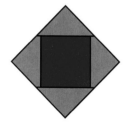
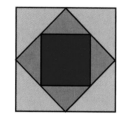

Refer to Option #1 and #3 for tips.

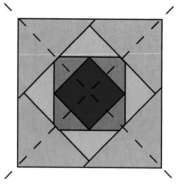

Chart for Option #13

Sewn Size of Corner Square	Cut for Center Square	Cut for First Row	Cut for Second Row	Cut for Third Row
1	3	1-3/4	2-1/4	3
1-1/4	3-1/2	2	3	3-3/4
1-1/2	4	2-1/4	3-1/4	4-1/4
1-3/4	4-1/2	2-1/2	3-1/2	4-3/4
2	5	2-3/4	3-3/4	5-1/4
2-1/4	5-1/2	3	4-1/4	5-3/4
2-1/2	6	3-1/4	4-1/2	6-1/4
3	7	3-3/4	5-1/4	6-3/4

Hint: remember sewn-finished or graph paper size are all the same size. Cut or raw edge is the same.

Sew a "SnS®" block. Sew around the block the first time and trim up to the point of the center square. Use one line on the ruler (90°) and place it over the seam, right up to the point. Be careful not to trim off too much or too little. This is like Option #4 and #10.

Figure strip size as always and sew around the block again leaving 1/4" seam allowance off of the tip like Option #1. Your inside square will now be blunted.

Figure new strip size and sew around your block for the 3rd time. Trim up to the tip, same as above, like Option #4.

Cut in half, twice, edge to edge, making sure you have 1/4" seam allowance on inside blunted square. Yields 4 units.

Hint: notice how a grid line will go through the bottom tip of the center square. This will help keep the block square.

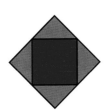
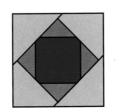
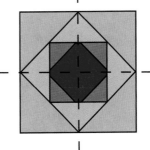

THIS CUT SIZE

Chart for Option #14

Cut Size of Square that will be 1/2 Square Triangles	Cut for Center Square	Cut for First Row	Cut for Second Row	Cut for Third Row
1	2	1-1/4	1-1/2	2-1/4
1-1/2	2-5/8	1-1/2	2	2-3/4
1-3/4	3	1-3/4	2-1/4	3
2	3-3/8	2	2-1/2	3-1/2
2-1/4	3-5/8	2-1/8	3	3-3/4
2-1/2	4	2-1/4	3-1/4	4-1/4
2-3/4	4-3/8	2-1/2	3-1/2	4-3/4
3	4-3/4	2-5/8	3-5/8	5
3-1/4	5	2-3/4	3-3/4	5-1/2
3-1/2	5-1/2	3	4-1/4	5-3/4

Math for Option #14: Draw your pattern out on graph paper. Measure the sewn size of your half square triangle. Multiply the desired cut size of that square triangle unit by 1.414, and add 1/2" to get the square size for the center square of your "SnS®". Round to the nearest 1/8". Figure corner strips as always.

For example: You want 3" half square triangles (finished size 2-1/2"). The center square is cut 4-3/4" or [(3" x 1.414) + 1/2"]. The corner strips are cut 2-3/8" (4-3/4" ÷ 2). Cut all four sides up to the point like the east and west sides on Option #3.

OPTION 15

Sew around your "SnS®" three times, cutting once edge to edge.

For this option, the block is trimmed differently. You will need to leave 1/4" seam allowance at the top and bottom of your "SnS®", the first time you sew around and trim up. On the opposite two sides of your square trim up to the point of inside center square. This is like Option #3 and #9.

Continue another row of strips around your "SnS®". Trim like Option #1 leaving 1/4" off each tip. Two sides will look like you cut and sewed the tips off. This is correct, don't fret!

Sew a 3rd row of strips on your "SnS®". Trimming will be like the Option #3 and #9 and like the starting paragraph from above. Make sure you trim up to the point on the block on the same sides as you did on your first row.

Cut in half across the open or flat tip corners yielding two units.

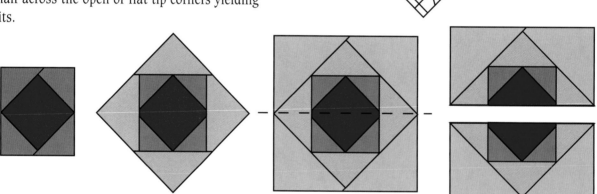

Chart for Option #15

For sewn size of inside rectangle flying goose	Cut for Center Square	Cut for First Row	Cut for Second Row	Cut for Third Row
1 x 2	2-1/4	1-3/8	1-3/4	2-1/2
1-1/4 x 2-1/2	2-5/8	1-5/8	2	2-3/4
1-1/2 x 3	3	1-3/4	2-1/4	3
1-3/4 x 3-1/2	3-3/8	2	2-1/2	3-1/2
2 x 4	3-3/4	2-1/8	2-3/4	3-3/4
2-1/4 x 4-1/2	4	2-1/4	3	4-1/4
2-1/2 x 5	4-3/8	2-1/2	3-1/4	4-3/4
2-3/4 x 5-1/2	4-3/4	2-5/8	3-1/2	5
3 x 6	5-1/8	2-7/8	4	5-3/4

Math for Option #15: Draw your pattern out on graph paper. Measure sewn center square and add 7/8" to the center square for cut size. Figure strip size as always.

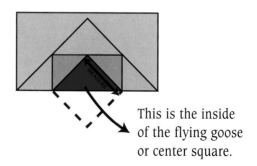

This is the inside of the flying goose or center square.

24

$\mathcal{O}$PTION 16

This new option is a mix of several options. You may choose anything to go in the center, to become the center square or unit. Try a pieced block, 4 patch, 9 patch, solid square...most anything will work. Next surround the center choice, like always, with the strip on each side of the center unit. Remember, only the center unit needs to be covered.

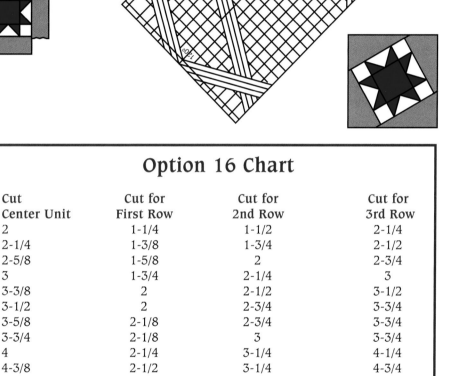

Place 60° angle over center unit. The 60° angle tip should lay over the tip of center unit, leaving 1/4" seam allowance off of the tip. Only one side of the ruler angle will line up with the seam below it. Trim all four corners, *rotate the block the same direction* as you trim it. All four corners should be turned clock wise or counter clockwise. This will create mirror images. Also be careful to always use the left side of the angle or the right when trimming all four corners. This will also create mirror image blocks. Practice with 2 blocks, cutting all four corners with the left, then the right side of the 60° angle on all four corners of the second block. This will help you see what you can create. The block will now start to twist. Sew around the block as many times as you need to design your block.

Option 16 Chart

Cut Center Unit	Cut for First Row	Cut for 2nd Row	Cut for 3rd Row
2	1-1/4	1-1/2	2-1/4
2-1/4	1-3/8	1-3/4	2-1/2
2-5/8	1-5/8	2	2-3/4
3	1-3/4	2-1/4	3
3-3/8	2	2-1/2	3-1/2
3-1/2	2	2-3/4	3-3/4
3-5/8	2-1/8	2-3/4	3-3/4
3-3/4	2-1/8	3	3-3/4
4	2-1/4	3-1/4	4-1/4
4-3/8	2-1/2	3-1/4	4-3/4
4-3/4	2-5/8	3-1/2	5
5	2-3/4	3-3/4	5-1/2
5-1/8	2-7/8	4	5-3/4
5-1/2	3	4-1/4	5-3/4
6	3-1/4	4-1/2	6-1/4
7	3-3/4	5-1/2	6-3/4

Hint: refer to option and option chart 1•2•5; it may help your designing

Hint: when the center unit is larger than a cut 5" or 6", 1/2" needs to be added, when figuring strip size, not the normal 1/4"

Hint: strip size may be rounded up for cutting to nearest 1/4".

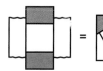 = = = = 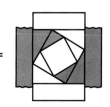 =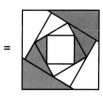

Keep sewing strips and trimming, block keeps twisting

The trisquare™ builds off of the option 4 half square triangle magic math™ and block. Four units are produced as this unit is sewn and cut. The center square is 2 equal width strips sewn together and cross cut into a square.

The center unit is now the center square and surrounded on each side, as all options are.

Trim right up to the tip on all 4 corners. Cut in half both directions.

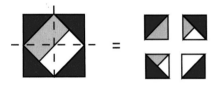

This will produce 4 equal units: 2 mirror image tri-squares™ and 2 half square triangles in 2 colors.

Design your quilt pattern to use all of the Option #17 units in the blocks and/or borders. To use the Option #17 chart, know the cut or sewn size of any of these units. Start with column 1 for cut size or column 2 for sewn measurement.

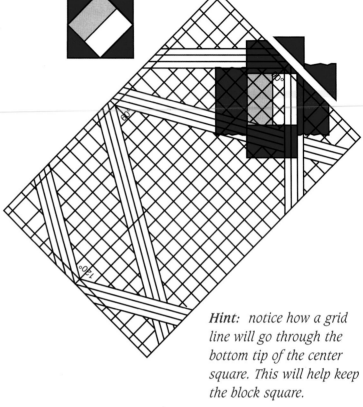

Hint: notice how a grid line will go through the bottom tip of the center square. This will help keep the block square.

 or *or*

Chart for Option #17

Cut or Raw Size	Sewn or Graph Paper Size	Cut 2 Strips	(crosscut to center unit size) Cut of Center Unit	Cut Strips & Sew Around Center Unit
1	1/2	1-1/4	2	1-1/4
1-1/4	3/4	1-3/8	2-1/4	1-1/4
1-1/2	1	1-5/8	2-5/8	1-1/2
1-3/4	1-1/4	1-3/4	3	1-3/4
2	1-1/2	1-7/8	3-3/8	2
2-1/4	1-3/4	2-1/8	3-5/8	2-1/8
2-1/2	2	2-1/4	4	2-1/4
2-3/4	2-1/4	2-1/2	4-3/8	2-1/2
3	2-1/2	2-5/8	4-3/4	2-5/8
3-1/4	2-3/4	2-7/8	5	2-3/4
3-1/2	3	3	5-1/2	3
3-3/4	3-1/4	3-1/4	6	3-1/4
4	3-1/2	3-3/8	6-1/4	3-1/2
4-1/2	4	3-3/4	6-7/8	4

Hint: refer to option and option chart 4 or 5. It may help your designing.

Use this math formula to find your strip size:

To find the strip size for the corner, measure center square...divide in half...add 1/4"... cut strip this measurement for the next row to sew around your square.

Hint: when the center unit is larger than a cut 5" or 6", 1/2" needs to be added, when figuring strip size, not the normal 1/4".

Hint: strip size may be rounded up for cutting to nearest 1/4".

$\mathscr{P}$ATTERN ADAPTING

For Pattern Adapting you will need:

- Notebook
- Calculator
- Graph Paper
- Colored Pencils
- Clear Ruler 1 x 12
- Pencil
- Quilt magazine or patterns you would like to adapt to Square in a Square®
- Square in a Square® Advancing On or Demonstration Charts for all options and Magic Math™ or Video or Borders By The Square

When you understand how to adapt patterns, and use the Magic Math, your opportunities are endless. This is quilt biology or how to break down the sections of construction. How to dissect a pattern or block or border and turn it into the options.

Pick a particular quilt and look at which options it would take to adapt it. Break it down or dissect it into the options. Decide what size block and draw it out on graph paper. After you have it drafted and the options chosen, you can work the math for that option to achieve the center square size. The strip size is then worked from the center square size.

If your pattern is available already drafted, you won't need to draw it again. If you don't have an accurate pattern, you will need to draft it.

Step 1:

Draw it out on graph paper. Use "quilt biology" and dissect the block into sections. Look for options (triangle units) that can be substituted for traditional triangles and squares. On occasion the option can be found when two of the blocks butt up next to each other. We call that the intersection. Now, redraw the block using the options in their proper location.

Now that the option is drawn, we need to find the size of the center square of each option. Refer to the options in your book. (All of the Magic Math™ and the 17 options can be found in Advancing on with Square in a Square®, the last half of the SnS Video or the demonstration spiral flip chart.) Each option will show you where the center square is with an X. You will need to refer to your pattern and get the required cut or sewn size to drop into the equation. Remember, we have a toll free number and are happy to help you.

Hint: remember sewn-finished or graph paper size is all the same measurement. Cut or raw edge is the same measurement.

Remember the video is an excellent way to learn the options, cutting and binding technique.

Traditional Pattern

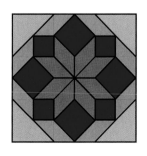
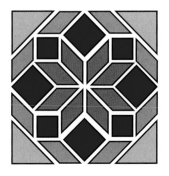

Using Options   Option #11   Option #1

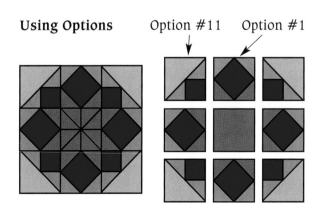

Step 2:

A. How to know the size of your quilt top: Decide how many blocks across the top and multiply that number by the graph paper size of your block.

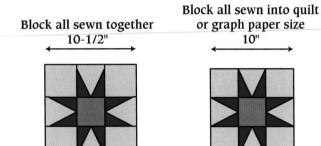

Block all sewn together 10-1/2"

Block all sewn into quilt or graph paper size 10"

You now know that the quilt is 50" across. Repeat for the number of rows down. Let's make ours 7 rows down. This quilt is now 50" x 70".

B. Do you want to add any sashing strips between your blocks? If so take the sewn or graph size of that strip and multiply it by how many rows you added. If we did that to our quilt it would be 4 rows x 2" = 8".

Cut 2-1/2"
Sewn 2"

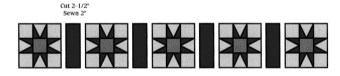

Going down would be 6 rows x 2" = 12.

Add that to our top.

50" across + 8" sashing = 58"
70" down + 12" sashing = 82"

C. Do you want a strip to go on each side of your quilt top? If so, add the sewn or graph paper size to the quilt top, bottom and each side. If ours was 2-1/2" cut, graph size is 2".

	Top	58"	
+		2"	top sashing or frame
+		2"	bottom sashing or frame
		62"	

	Down	82"	
+		2"	top sashing or frame
+		2"	bottom sashing or frame
		86"	

Our quilt top is now 62" x 86", (that is sewn or graph measurement). With seam allowance the quilt top is 62-1/2" x 86-1/2".

If you were actually making this quilt and had measured the top it would be 62-1/2" x 86-1/2".

Step 3:

A. How to do the border? The easiest way would be to pick the option you wanted and use the option chart. But, we will start at the beginning.

  a. Pick the option. Example: Option #3

  b. Know graph size of quilt top. Example: 62" x 86"

  c. Find a number that equally goes into that. Example: 2". That would make 31 flying geese for the top and 43 for the side. Sew in a traditional flying geese pattern.

  If you choose an end to end design as shown you will have:
  62 ÷ 4 = 15.5 (top)
  86 ÷ 4 = 21.5 (each side)

  Now we need to figure out how to work in the .5 or 1/2". The 1/2" in this example can be worked in to make the border strip wider on each side. In that case you would add 1/4" to each side to take up the 1/2". The 1/2" can also be used as the corner square if your border is 1/2" wide. You won't be perfect on your cutting or sewing. A small amount can be worked in.

D. The Option #3 Flying Geese yields 2 units. We need to know how many to make for the border. The math you did on Step 3 told you

> 15   top
> 15   bottom
> 21   side
> <u>21</u>   side
> 72   =   total geese units

> 72 ÷ 2 = 36 Option #3 units

Sew 36 Option #3s. If you don't have the Option #3 chart to tell you your option center square measurement or strip size, then draw on graph paper a 2 x 4 goose. Measure from wing tip (the bold line) down to tip and add 7/8" = center square size.

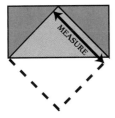

Next you would sew 15 units end to end. Sew one for the top and one for the bottom.

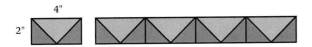

E. If you wanted to sew the geese in traditional flying geese formation, do the same math as above except use the end measurement of your geese and not the length measurement.

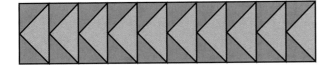

F. Your quilt top now looks like this:

15 UNITS, OPTION #3 BORDER END TO END

BLOCKS & SASHING

Notice you have empty holes in each corner. You may put a solid 2" (cut 2-1/2") square there or add one extra goose to 2 sides.

Quilt Border Planning
Familiarize yourself with and master the Square in a Square® technique. Become acquainted with the options used to create the block or pattern or border. View the video so you can have the big picture.

To figure fabric amounts you will need:

- scratch paper
- calculator
- pencil
- quilt pattern - drafted to graph paper and adapted to Square in a Square®
- fabric charts from page 31-34

Step 1:

Take your drawn pattern and mark your measurements in the units

BLOCK SIZE • CUT 4-1/2 • SEWN 4

E
X
A
M
P
L
E

Cut 2-1/2'

A → Cut 1-1/2"

B → Cut 2-1/4"

C → Cut 1-3/8"

→ Cut 2-1/2"

D

Step 2:

Each unit in the block will need to be broken down into squares, strips and blocks.

Example: Unit A is a solid cut square - 1-1/2". You need to know how many 1-1/2" squares can be cut out of a strip. (Check the Strip Chart on page 32) Divide the number in the strip length 40" ÷ 1.5 = 26 squares. That is 39" with one 1" left over.

How many A squares do you need in the block? The answer is 4. Divide 4 units into the number of squares per strip 39 ÷ 4 = 3 blocks with 3 left over.

Know how many blocks are in the quilt you wish to make. Lets say 12. 3 blocks in a strip is 12 ÷ 3 = 4.

You need to cut 4 strips. Multiply the strip by how wide the strip is cut. 1.50 4 x 1.50 = 6". That number is the amount of fabric you need to purchase if you were making a large number of blocks. Remember that 1 - 1/2" square is left out of each strip, so every 4 strips you get enough for 1 total block.

HELPFUL HINTS

- A strip of fabric is cut selvage to selvage from yard goods. We figure a 40" average from our strips.

- When rounding the numbers, round up.

- For best use of fabric cut the largest amounts first and work down to the smallest.

- Some small cuts can be cut from the left overs of the large cut.

- If you are concerned about running out of a fabric and the color placement would work for the option and block, use the least amount of yardage for the center square of your option unit. This usually works really well for "Option 4", half square triangles.

- If you are concerned about running low on a fabric and it is an option where you trim up to the tip, (like "Option #4"), your strips can be figured in length, right up to the tip. It will look too short, but when trimmed it is perfect!

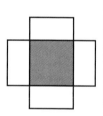

- A quick comment on the strip length: To get the most out of your fabric when figuring option strips: Take your cut center square size, add 1/4" to each end 2-1/4 would be 2-3/4: multiply times 4 (each side of the center square) This is how many inches you need to go around your square. Rounding up is easy to figure. I normally round up to the closest whole or 1/2 number. I would round up to 3" in the case of the example 2-1/4" center square.

2-3/4" ← 2-1/4" → 2-3/4"

Step 3:

How to figure fabric for your options. Figure the center square (B) as you would for a solid square. Like above, Step 2. Next, how many options in the block? The example block has 4 star point units = flying geese: This unit is "Option #3", 2 flying geese.

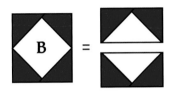

You would need 2 "Option #3s" = 4 star points. That means 2 squares 2-1/4". Multiply 4 sides x square size = 9" that is the actual amount you would need to cover each side of your square. With this technique you want to cut your strips a little longer than your square, for speed chain piecing.

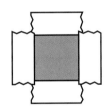

I would round the 2-1/4" block to a 3", to cover each side. Then, multiply the 3" x 4 sides = 12". Each option will take 12", divided into strip length 40 ÷ 12 = 3 with 4" left over. In this case that 4" will be another option with every 3 strips cut. Three and a third options out of one 1-3/8" x 40" strip. If 12 blocks are needed, divide the 3-1/3 into blocks needed. That tells you 4 strips need to be cut 1-3/8" wide, 4 x 1-3/8" = 5-1/2" or 1/4 yard fabric.

How many inches per yardage?

1/8 yd.	=	4-1/2"	=	.125
1/4 yd.	=	9"	=	.25
1/3 yd.	=	12"	=	.34
1/2 yd.	=	18"	=	.5
5/8 yd.	=	22-1/2"	=	.625
2/3 yd.	=	24"	=	.67
3/4 yd.	=	27"	=	.75
1 yd.	=	36"		

Chart for Backing Fabric

Quilt Size	Fig #	Amount	2-1/2" Binding
Twin 63 x 87	1	5-1/4	3/4 yd.
Double 78 x 87	1	5-1/4	3/4 yd.
Queen 84 x 92	2	7-1/2	7/8 yd.
King 100 x 92	3	8	1 yd.

Fig. 1

Fig. 2

Fig. 3

FABRIC INFORMATION

Rounding and estimating is used for figuring the fabric amounts. It is also used in figuring strip quantities, for the block charts. You may need more or less depending on your own style of spacing, trimming, cutting and sewing.

Strips that are sewn around the center square are corner strips or surround strips. You will need to know how many options will yield from the strip. Total the 4 sides of the center square and add 1", divide that into the 40" average of a strip, selvedge to selvedge.

How Many Strips in a Yard:

36	-	1"	strips in 1 yard
24	-	1-1/2"	strips in 1 yard
18	-	2"	strips in 1 yard
14	-	2-1/2"	strips in 1 yard
12	-	3"	strips in 1 yard
10	-	3-1/2"	strips in 1 yard
9	-	4"	strips in 1 yard

Strip Width	Options	Material Left Over
4" total surround strip	10	-
5" total surround strip	8	-
6" total surround strip	6	4"
8" total surround strip	5	4"
12" total surround strip	3	4"
14" total surround strip	2	12"
16" total surround strip	2	4"
20" total surround strip	2	

How Many Squares in a 40" Strip:

40	-	1"	squares
32	-	1-1/4"	squares
26	-	1-1/2"	squares
22	-	1-3/4"	squares
20	-	2"	squares
17	-	2-1/4"	squares
16	-	2-1/2"	squares
14	-	2-3/4"	squares
13	-	3"	squares
12	-	3-1/4"	squares
11	-	3-1/2"	squares
10	-	3-3/4"	squares
10	-	4"	squares
9	-	4-1/4"	squares
8	-	4-1/2"	squares
8	-	4-3/4"	squares
8	-	5"	squares

TIPS

- Remember to sew a "scant" 1/4" seam
- Spray starch helps to keep washed fabric from moving.
- A finger space between the square on the strip is all that's needed, when sewing the basic square.
- Blunt corners are good.
- Use short strips on both side 3 and side 4 when sewing the basic square.
- If your option is too large or small, check:
  1. center square size
  2. seam allowance
  3. the way you lay your ruler on the sewn square.

Fabric Estimated Strips

How many strips per width in a segment

(Small cleanup cuts may be included.)

4	-	1"	strip	in	1/8	yard	=	4-1/2"	=	.125
8	-	1"	strip	in	1/4	yard	=	9"	=	.25
11	-	1"	strip	in	1/3	yard	=	12"	=	.34
16	-	1"	strip	in	1/2	yard	=	18"	=	.50
20	-	1"	strip	in	5/8	yard	=	22-1/2"	=	.625
20	-	1"	strip	in	2/3	yard	=	24"	=	.67
24	-	1"	strip	in	3/4	yard	=	27"	=	.75
34	-	1"	strip	in	1	yard	=	36"	=	1.00
3	-	1-1/4"	strip	in	1/8	yard	=	4-1/2"	=	.125
7	-	1-1/4"	strip	in	1/4	yard	=	9"	=	.25
9	-	1-1/4"	strip	in	1/3	yard	=	12"	=	.34
14	-	1-1/4"	strip	in	1/2	yard	=	18"	=	.50
17	-	1-1/4"	strip	in	5/8	yard	=	22-1/2"	=	.625
18	-	1-1/4"	strip	in	2/3	yard	=	24"	=	.67
21	-	1-1/4"	strip	in	3/4	yard	=	27"	=	.75
28	-	1-1/2"	strip	in	1	yard	=	36"	=	1.00
2	-	1-1/2"	strip	in	1/8	yard	=	4-1/2"	=	.125
5	-	1-1/2"	strip	in	1/4	yard	=	9"	=	.25
7	-	1-1/2"	strip	in	1/3	yard	=	12"	=	.34
11	-	1-1/2"	strip	in	1/2	yard	=	18"	=	.50
14	-	1-1/2"	strip	in	5/8	yard	=	22-1/2"	=	.625
15	-	1-1/2"	strip	in	2/3	yard	=	24"	=	.67
17	-	1-1/2"	strip	in	3/4	yard	=	27"	=	.75
22	-	1-1/2"	strip	in	1	yard	=	36"	=	1.00
2	-	2"	strip	in	1/8	yard	=	4-1/2"	=	.125
4	-	2"	strip	in	1/4	yard	=	9"	=	.25
5	-	2"	strip	in	1/3	yard	=	12"	=	.34
8	-	2"	strip	in	1/2	yard	=	18"	=	.50
10	-	2"	strip	in	5/8	yard	=	22-1/2"	=	.625
11	-	2"	strip	in	2/3	yard	=	24"	=	.67
12	-	2"	strip	in	3/4	yard	=	27"	=	.75
17	-	2"	strip	in	1	yard	=	36"	=	1.00
1	-	2-1/2"	strip	in	1/8	yard	=	4-1/2"	=	.125
3	-	2-1/2"	strip	in	1/4	yard	=	9"	=	.25
4	-	2-1/2"	strip	in	1/3	yard	=	12"	=	.34
7	-	2-1/2"	strip	in	1/2	yard	=	18"	=	.50
9	-	2-1/2"	strip	in	5/8	yard	=	22-1/2"	=	.625
10	-	2-1/2"	strip	in	2/3	yard	=	24"	=	.67
11	-	2-1/2"	strip	in	3/4	yard	=	27"	=	.75
14	-	2-1/2"	strip	in	1	yard	=	36"	=	1.00

Fabric Estimated Strips, *continued*

1	-	3"	strip	in	1/8	yard	=	4-1/2"	=	.125
2	-	3"	strip	in	1/4	yard	=	9"	=	.25
3	-	3"	strip	in	1/3	yard	=	12"	=	.34
5	-	3"	strip	in	1/2	yard	=	18"	=	.50
7	-	3"	strip	in	5/8	yard	=	22-1/2"	=	.625
7	-	3"	strip	in	2/3	yard	=	24"	=	.67
8	-	3"	strip	in	3/4	yard	=	27"	=	.75
11	-	3"	strip	in	1	yard	=	36"	=	1.00
1	-	4"	strip	in	1/8	yard	=	4-1/2"	=	.125
2	-	4"	strip	in	1/4	yard	=	9"	=	.25
3	-	4"	strip	in	1/3	yard	=	12"	=	.34
4	-	4"	strip	in	1/2	yard	=	18"	=	.50
5	-	4"	strip	in	5/8	yard	=	22-1/2"	=	.625
6	-	4"	strip	in	2/3	yard	=	24"	=	.67
6	-	4"	strip	in	3/4	yard	=	27"	=	.75
9	-	4"	strip	in	1	yard	=	36"	=	1.00
0	-	5"	strip	in	1/8	yard	=	4-1/2"	=	.125
1	-	5"	strip	in	1/4	yard	=	9"	=	.25
2	-	5"	strip	in	1/3	yard	=	12"	=	.34
3	-	5"	strip	in	1/2	yard	=	18"	=	.50
4	-	5"	strip	in	5/8	yard	=	22-1/2"	=	.625
4	-	5"	strip	in	2/3	yard	=	24"	=	.67
5	-	5"	strip	in	3/4	yard	=	27"	=	.75
7	-	5"	strip	in	1	yard	=	36"	=	1.00

These Option Charts will help you know the cut center square size and cut strip size for the requested option unit. Refer to individual options for details or know the unit size you require. Remember, sewn-finished, or graph paper size is one measurement and cut or raw edge is a larger measurement. Learning how to use the Option Charts will eliminate the Magic Math and get you going on the creating of your own design.

Chart for Option #1
Total Finished Size

Sewn-Finished or Graph Paper Size	Cut Center Square	Cut Strip Size
1	1-1/4	3/4
1-1/4	1-3/8	1
1-1/2	1-5/8	1-1/8
1-3/4	1-3/4	1-1/4
2	2	1-1/4
2-1/4	2-1/8	1-3/8
2-1/2	2-1/4	1-3/8
2-3/4	2-1/2	1-1/2
3	2-5/8	1-5/8
3-1/4	2-3/4	1-5/8
3-1/2	3	1-3/4
3-3/4	3-1/8	1-7/8
4	3-3/8	1-7/8
4-1/4	3-1/2	2
4-1/2	3-5/8	2-1/8
4-3/4	3-7/8	2-1/4
5	4	2-1/4

Chart for Option #2

Sewn-Finished or Graph Paper Size	Cut Center Square	Cut 1st Strip	Cut 2nd Strip
2	1-1/2	1	1-1/8
2-1/4	1-5/8	1	1-1/4
2-1/2	1-3/4	1-1/8	1-3/8
2-3/4	1-7/8	1-1/4	1-1/2
3	2	1-1/4	1-1/2
3-1/4	2-1/8	1-3/8	1-5/8
3-1/2	2-1/4	1-3/8	1-3/4
3-3/4	2-3/8	1-1/2	1-7/8
4	2-1/2	1-1/2	1-7/8
4-1/4	2-5/8	1-5/8	2
4-1/2	2-3/4	1-3/4	2-1/4
4-3/4	2-7/8	1-3/4	2-1/4
5	3	1-3/4	2-1/4

Chart for Option #3
Flying Geese

For Sewn Size of Rectangle Unit	Cut Center Square	Cut Strip Size
1 x 2	2-1/4	1-3/8
1-1/4 x 2-1/2	2-5/8	1-5/8
1-1/2 x 3	3	1-3/4
1-3/4 x 3-1/2	3-3/8	2
2 x 4	3-3/4	2-1/8
2-1/4 x 4-1/2	4	2-1/4
2-1/2 x 5	4-3/8	2-1/2
2-3/4 x 5-1/2	4-3/4	2-5/8
3 x 6	5-1/8	2-7/8

Chart for Option #4
Half Square Triangles

For Sewn Size of 1/2 Square Triangle Unit	Cut Center Square	Cut Strip Size
1/2	2	1-1/4
1	2-5/8	1-1/2
1-1/4	3	1-3/4
1-1/2	3-3/8	2
1-3/4	3-5/8	2-1/8
2	4	2-1/4
2-1/4	4-3/8	2-1/2
2-1/2	4-3/4	2-5/8
2-3/4	5	2-3/4
3	5-1/2	3

Chart for Option #5
Total Finished Size

Sewn-Finished or Graph Paper Size	Cut Center Square	Cut Strip Size
1	1-1/4	3/4
1-1/4	1-3/8	1
1-1/2	1-5/8	1-1/8
1-3/4	1-3/4	1-1/4
2	2	1-1/4
2-1/4	2-1/8	1-3/8
2-1/2	2-1/4	1-3/8
2-3/4	2-1/2	1-1/2
3	2-5/8	1-5/8
3-1/4	2-3/4	1-5/8
3-1/2	3	1-3/4
3-3/4	3-1/8	1-7/8
4	3-3/8	1-7/8
4-1/4	3-1/2	2
4-1/2	3-5/8	2-1/8
4-3/4	3-7/8	2-1/4
5	4	2-1/4

Chart for Option #7

Sewn-Finished or Graph Paper Size Rectangle	Cut Strip for center Diamond	Cut Strip Size
1 x 1-3/4	1-3/8	1
1-1/4 x 2	1-1/2	1
1-1/2 x 2-1/2	1-3/4	1-1/8
1-3/4 x 3	2	1-1/4
2 x 3-1/2	2-1/4	1-3/8
2-1/4 x 4	2-1/2	1-1/2
2-1/2 x 4-1/4	2-3/4	1-5/8
2-3/4 x 4-5/8	2-7/8	1-3/4
3 x 5-1/4	3-1/4	1-7/8
3-1/4 x 5-3/4	3-3/8	2
3-1/2 x 6-1/4	3-1/2	2
3-3/4 x 6-5/8	3-3/4	2-1/8
4 x 7	4	2-1/4
4-1/4 x 7-1/2	4-1/4	2-3/8

Chart for Option #8

Sewn Corner Square Size	Cut Center Square	Strip Size
1	3	1-3/4
1-1/4	3-1/2	2
1-1/2	4	2-1/4
1-3/4	4-1/2	2-1/2
2	5	2-3/4
2-1/4	5-1/2	3
2-1/2	6	3-1/4
2-3/4	6-1/2	3-1/2
3	7	3-3/4

Chart for Option #9 - Flying Geese

For Sewn Size of inside rectangle flying goose	Cut Center Square	Cut Strip Size For 1st Row	Cut Strip Size For 2nd Row
1 x 2	2-1/4	1-3/8	1-3/4
1-1/4 x 2-1/2	2-5/8	1-5/8	2
1-1/2 x 3	3	1-3/4	2-1/4
1-3/4 x 3-1/2	3-3/8	2	2-1/2
2 x 4	3-3/4	2-1/8	2-3/4
2-1/4 x 4-1/2	4	2-1/4	3
2-1/2 x 5	4-3/8	2-1/2	3-1/4
2-3/4 x 5-1/2	4-3/4	2-5/8	3-1/2
3 x 6	5-1/8	2-7/8	4

Chart for Option #10

Cut Size of Square that will be 1/2 Square Triangles	Cut for Center Square	Cut for First Row	Cut for Second Row
1	2	1-1/4	1-1/2
1-1/2	2-5/8	1-1/2	2
1-3/4	3	1-3/4	2-1/4
2	3-3/8	2	2-1/2
2-1/4	3-5/8	2-1/8	3
2-1/2	4	2-1/4	3-1/4
2-3/4	4-3/8	2-1/2	3-1/2
3	4-3/4	2-5/8	3-5/8
3-1/4	5	2-3/4	3-3/4
3-1/2	5-1/2	3	4-1/4

Chart for Option #11

Sewn Size of Corner Square	Cut for Center Square	Cut for First Row	Cut for Second Row
1	3	1-3/4	2-1/4
1-1/4	3-1/2	2	3
1-1/2	4	2-1/4	3-1/4
1-3/4	4-1/2	2-1/2	3-1/2
2	5	2-3/4	3-3/4
2-1/4	5-1/2	3	4-1/4
2-1/2	6	3-1/4	4-1/2
3	7	3-3/4	5-1/4

Trip Around The Star
67" x 90"

Summer Breeze
58" x 58"

Moody Blues
32" x 40"

Pineapple Diamond
38" x 42"

Ohio Star
36" x 40"

Pineapple Picnic
44" x 53"

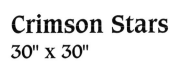

Crimson Stars
30" x 30"

We Will Never Forget
69" x 80"

Sassy Star
19.5" x 43"

Sassy Star II
19.5" x 60"

Christmas Star
32" x 32"

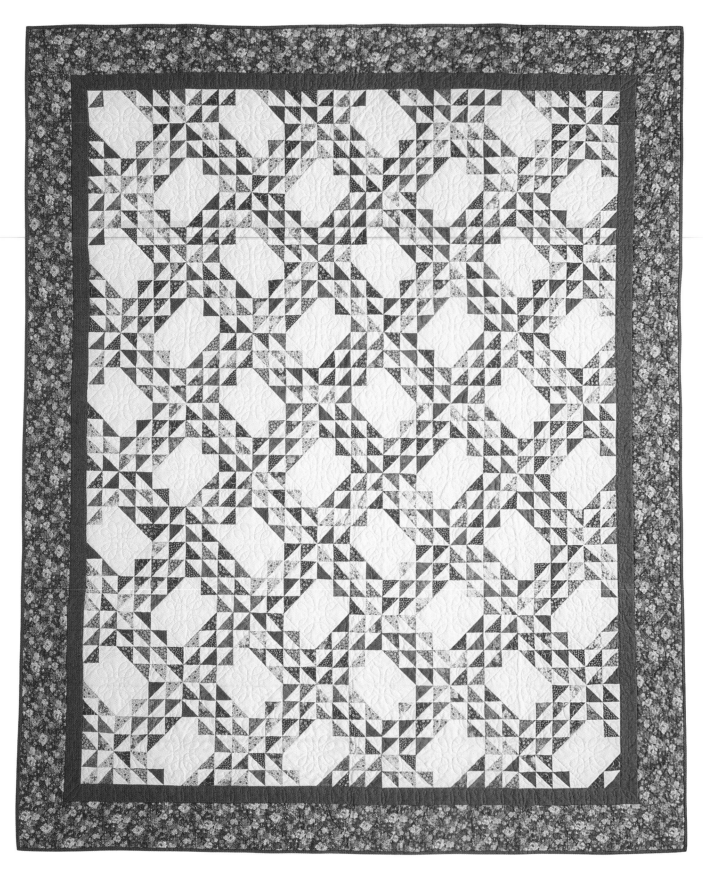

Waves of Love
79" x 85"

Chinese Lanterns
24" x 30"

In The Garden With Tumbling Blocks
38" x 42"

Shirttails
32" x 40"

Chart for Option #13

Sewn Size of Corner Square	Cut for Center Square	Cut for First Row	Cut for Second Row	Cut for Third Row
1	3	1-3/4	2-1/4	3
1-1/4	3-1/2	2	3	3-3/4
1-1/2	4	2-1/4	3-1/4	4-1/4
1-3/4	4-1/2	2-1/2	3-1/2	4-3/4
2	5	2-3/4	3-3/4	5-1/4
2-1/4	5-1/2	3	4-1/4	5-3/4
2-1/2	6	3-1/4	4-1/2	6-1/4
3	7	3-3/4	5-1/4	6-3/4

Chart for Option #14

Cut Size of Square that will be 1/2 Square Triangles	Cut for Center Square	Cut for First Row	Cut for Second Row	Cut for Third Row
1	2	1-1/4	1-1/2	2-1/4
1-1/2	2-5/8	1-1/2	2	2-3/4
1-3/4	3	1-3/4	2-1/4	3
2	3-3/8	2	2-1/2	3-1/2
2-1/4	3-5/8	2-1/8	3	3-3/4
2-1/2	4	2-1/4	3-1/4	4-1/4
2-3/4	4-3/8	2-1/2	3-1/2	4-3/4
3	4-3/4	2-5/8	3-5/8	5
3-1/4	5	2-3/4	3-3/4	5-1/2
3-1/2	5-1/2	3	4-1/4	5-3/4

Chart for Option #15

For sewn size of inside rectangle flying goose	Cut for Center Square	Cut for First Row	Cut for Second Row	Cut for Third Row
1 x 2	2-1/4	1-3/8	1-3/4	2-1/2
1-1/4 x 2-1/2	2-5/8	1-5/8	2	2-3/4
1-1/2 x 3	3	1-3/4	2-1/4	3
1-3/4 x 3-1/2	3-3/8	2	2-1/2	3-1/2
2 x 4	3-3/4	2-1/8	2-3/4	3-3/4
2-1/4 x 4-1/2	4	2-1/4	3	4-1/4
2-1/2 x 5	4-3/8	2-1/2	3-1/4	4-3/4
2-3/4 x 5-1/2	4-3/4	2-5/8	3-1/2	5
3 x 6	5-1/8	2-7/8	4	5-3/4

Chart for Option #16

Cut Center Unit	Cut for First Row	Cut for 2nd Row	Cut for 3rd Row
2	1-1/4	1-1/2	2-1/4
2-1/4	1-3/8	1-3/4	2-1/2
2-5/8	1-5/8	2	2-3/4
3	1-3/4	2-1/4	3
3-3/8	2	2-1/2	3-1/2
3-1/2	2	2-3/4	3-3/4
3-5/8	2-1/8	2-3/4	3-3/4
3-3/4	2-1/8	3	3-3/4
4	2-1/4	3-1/4	4-1/4
4-3/8	2-1/2	3-1/4	4-3/4
4-3/4	2-5/8	3-1/2	5
5	2-3/4	3-3/4	5-1/2
5-1/8	2-7/8	4	5-3/4
5-1/2	3	4-1/4	5-3/4
6	3-1/4	4-1/2	6-1/4
7	3-3/4	5-1/2	6-3/4

Chart for Option #17

Cut or Raw Size	Sewn or Graph Paper Size	Cut 2 Strips	(crosscut to center unit size) Cut of Center Unit	Cut Strips & Sew Around Center Unit
1	1/2	1-1/4	2	1-1/4
1-1/4	3/4	1-3/8	2-1/4	1-1/4
1-1/2	1	1-5/8	2-5/8	1-1/2
1-3/4	1-1/4	1-3/4	3	1-3/4
2	1-1/2	1-7/8	3-3/8	2
2-1/4	1-3/4	2-1/8	3-5/8	2-1/8
2-1/2	2	2-1/4	4	2-1/4
2-3/4	2-1/4	2-1/2	4-3/8	2-1/2
3	2-1/2	2-5/8	4-3/4	2-5/8
3-1/4	2-3/4	2-7/8	5	2-3/4
3-1/2	3	3	5-1/2	3
3-3/4	3-1/4	3-1/4	6	3-1/4
4	3-1/2	3-3/8	6-1/4	3-1/2
4-1/2	4	3-3/4	6-7/8	4

44

Option #8 Chart as Corner Units

When you need an Option 8 unit in the corners of the block design, know the sewn size of the unit in the center of your design and match up with Option 8 corner. The chart will tell you the cut center size of the Option 8 and surround strip width. Remember, you can use anything solid or pieced as your center unit of block design.

HINT: Review Option 8 cutting and sewing.

HINT: As the center option square becomes 6" or larger, you may need to add 1/2" to strip measurement on the surround strips magic math, not the common 1/4".

Sewn Block Center Design	Option 8 Cut Center Square	Option 8 Strip Cut Size
2"	2-1/2"	1-1/2"
3"	3"	1-3/4"
4"	3-3/4"	2-1/4"
5"	4-1/2"	2-1/2"
6"	5-1/2"	3-1/4"
7"	6"	3-1/2"
8"	6-3/4"	3-3/4"

Option 8 unit

Center unit as a 9 patch sewn size 6" cut with raw edge 6-1/2"

Option #9 Chart as Corner Units

When you need an Option 9 unit in the corners of the block design, or matching up to a square unit. Know the sewn size of the unit in the center of your design that is a square and the Option 9 is matching up to. The chart will tell you the cut center square size of the Option 9 and the 2 rows of surround strips. Remember, you can use any thing solid or pieced as your center unit of block design.

HINT: Review Option 9 cutting and sewing.

HINT: As the center option square becomes 6" or larger, you may need to add 1/2" to strip measurement on the surround strips magic math, not the common 1/4".

Sewn Block Center Design	Option 9 Cut Center Square	Row 1 Strip Cut Size	Row 2 Strip Cut Size
2"	1-1/2"	1"	1-1/4"
3"	1-7/8"	1-1/8"	1-1/2"
4"	2-1/4"	1-3/8"	1-3/4"
5"	2-5/8"	1-5/8"	2"
6"	3"	1-3/4"	2-1/4"
7"	3-3/8"	2"	2-1/2"
8"	3-3/4"	2-1/8"	2-3/4"

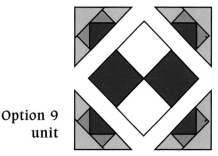

Option 9 unit

Center unit as a 4 patch sewn size 6" cut with raw edge 6-1/2"

Option #10 Chart to Match Corners of Square Unit or Block

When you need an Option 10 unit in the corners of the block design, or matching up to a square unit. Know the sewn size of the unit in the center of your design that is a square and the Option 10 that is matching up to it. The chart will tell you the cut center square size of the Option 10 and the 2 rows of surround strips. Remember, you can use any thing solid or pieced as your center unit of block design.

HINT: Review Option 10 cutting and sewing.

Total Pieced Block			Center of Pieced Block Solid Unit or Pieced Unit			Cut Center Square for Option 10 unit	Row 1 Strip Cut Size	Row 2 Strip Cut Size
Cut	Sewn	-	Cut	Sewn	-			
4-1/2"	4"	-	3-3/8"	2-7/8"	-	2-5/8"	1-1/2"	2"
6-1/2"	6"	-	4-3/4"	4-1/4"	-	3-3/8"	2"	2-1/2"
8-1/2"	8"	-	6-1/4"	5-3/4"	-	4"	2-1/4"	3-1/4"
10-1/2"	10"	-	7-1/2"	7"	-	4-3/4"	2-5/8"	3-5/8"
12-1/2"	12"	-	9"	8-1/2"	-	5-1/2"	3"	4-1/4"

Your design may require an Option #1, connecting to an Option #3 to create the pattern.

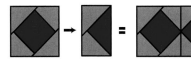 OR

Know Option #1 sewn size, column 1, and follow to the right through each column to know option center square cut size and cut strip size.

Option 1's Equal to Same Size Option 3			Option 3 — Match up to Option 1 on the same row	
Sewn-Finished or Graph Paper Size	Cut Center Square	Cut Strip Size	Flying Goose Cut Center Square	Flying Goose Cut Strip Size
1	1-1/4	3/4	1-5/8	1-1/8
1-1/4	1-3/8	1	1-3/4	1-1/4
1-1/2	1-5/8	1-1/8	2	1-1/4
1-3/4	1-3/4	1-1/4	2-1/8	1-3/8
2	2	1-1/4	2-3/8	1-3/8
2-1/4	2-1/8	1-3/8	2-1/2	1-1/2
2-1/2	2-1/4	1-3/8	2-5/8	1-5/8
2-3/4	2-1/2	1-1/2	2-7/8	1-5/8
3	2-5/8	1-5/8	3	1-3/4
3-1/4	2-3/4	1-5/8	3-1/8	1-7/8
3-1/2	3	1-3/4	3-3/8	2
3-3/4	3-1/8	1-7/8	3-1/2	2
4	3-3/8	1-7/8	3-3/4	2-1/8
4-1/4	3-1/2	2	3-7/8	2-1/4
4-1/2	3-5/8	2-1/8	4	2-1/4
4-3/4	3-7/8	2-1/4	4-1/4	2-3/8
5	4	2-1/4	4-3/8	2-1/2

Many times for a design you will need an option to match up to another unit.
This chart shows how an Option #1 matches up to a 4-Patch unit. Find the size you need
and follow through to the right for matching units.

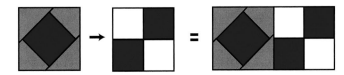

Chart for Option #1
and Matching 4 patch

Option 1 Cut or Raw Size	Sewn-Finished or Graph Paper Size	Cut Center Square	Cut Strip Size	4 Patch Cut Strip or Square Size (these must be cut exact)
1-1/2	1	1-1/4	3/4	1
1-3/4	1-1/4	1-3/8	1	1-1/8
2	1-1/2	1-5/8	1-1/8	1-1/4
2-1/4	1-3/4	1-3/4	1-1/4	1-3/8
2-1/2	2	2	1-1/4	1-1/2
2-3/4	2-1/4	2-1/8	1-3/8	1-5/8
3	2-1/2	2-1/4	1-3/8	1-3/4
3-1/4	2-3/4	2-1/2	1-1/2	1-7/8
3-1/2	3	2-5/8	1-5/8	2
3-3/4	3-1/4	2-3/4	1-5/8	2-1/8
4	3-1/2	3	1-3/4	2-1/4
4-1/4	3-3/4	3-1/8	1-7/8	2-3/8
4-1/2	4	3-3/8	1-7/8	2-1/2
4-3/4	4-1/4	3-1/2	2	2-5/8
5	4-1/2	3-5/8	2-1/8	2-3/4
5-1/4	4-3/4	3-7/8	2-1/4	2-7/8
5-1/2	5	4	2-1/4	3

This chart shows how an Option #3 (flying geese) matches to an Option #4 (half square triangle).

Use half square triangle unit on the left side or right side as needed

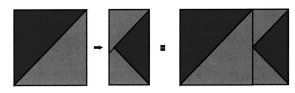

Know sewn size of flying goose unit (third column)

Chart for Option #3
Matching Option #4

Half square triangles matching up to the **short** side of sewn flying geese		For Option #3 Sewn Size	Cut Center Square	Cut Strip Size	Half square triangles matching up to the **long** side of sewn flying geese	
Cut Option 4 Center Square	Cut Strip Size				Cut Option #4 Center Square	Cut Strip Size
2-5/8	1-1/2	1 x 2	2-1/4	1-3/8	4	2-1/4
3	1-3/4	1-1/4 x 2-1/2	2-5/8	1-5/8	4-3/4	2-5/8
3-3/8	2	1-1/2 x 3	3	1-3/4	5-1/2	3
3-5/8	2-1/8	1-3/4 x 3-1/2	3-3/8	2	6-1/8	3-3/8
4	2-1/4	2 x 4	3-3/4	2-1/8	6-7/8	3-3/4
4-3/8	2-1/2	2-1/4 x 4-1/2	4	2-1/4		
4-3/4	2-5/8	2-1/2 x 5	4-3/8	2-1/2		
5	2-3/4	2-3/4 x 5-1/2	4-3/4	2-5/8		
5-1/2	3	3 x 6	5-1/8	2-7/8		

This chart shows how an Option #3 (flying geese) matches to a solid rectangle unit.

Know one of the above sizes - find it on the chart and follow across.

Chart for Option #3 Flying Geese
Matching a Solid Rectangle

Cut or raw edge size of flying geese unit	Flying Geese For Sewn Size	For Option 3 Cut Center Square	For Option 3 Cut Strip Size	Cut Rectangle Unit Size	Fabric Amounts for Solid Rectangle Units		
1-1/2 x 2-1/2	1 x 2	2-1/4	1-3/8	1-1/2 x 2-1/2	1 strip	16 units	4 blocks
1-3/4 x 3	1-1/4 x 2-1/2	2-5/8	1-5/8	1-3/4 x 3	1 strip	13 units	3 blocks
2 x 3-1/2	1-1/2 x 3	3	1-3/4	2 x 3-1/2	1 strip	11 units	3 blocks
2-1/4 x 4	1-3/4 x 3-1/2	3-3/8	2	2-1/4 x 4	1 strip	10 units	2.5 blocks
2-1/2 x 4-1/2	2 x 4	3-3/4	2-1/8	2-1/2 x 4-1/2	1 strip	8 units	2 blocks
2-3/4 x 4	2-1/4 x 4-1/2	4	2-1/4	2-3/4 x 4	1 strip	8 units	2 blocks
3 x 5-1/2	2-1/2 x 5	4-3/8	2-1/2	3 x 5-1/2	1 strip	8 units	2 blocks
3-1/4 x 6	2-3/4 x 5-1/2	4-3/4	2-5/8	3-1/4 x 6	1 strip	6 units	1 blocks
3-1/2 x 6-1/2	3 x 6	5-1/8	2-7/8	3-1/2 x 6-1/2	1 strip	6 units	1 blocks

This chart shows how a solid square matches to an Option #1 - match to Option #3 - match to a Pinwheel.

Chart for Solid Square Matching up to
Option #1 or Option #3 or Pinwheel

Cut Solid Square	Sewn Solid Square	Opt 1 Sewn-Finished or Graph Paper Size	Option 1 Cut Center Square	Option 1 Cut Strip Size	Flying Goose Cut Center Square	Flying Goose Cut Strip Size	Cut Center Square Size for Option 4 Half Square Triangles	Cut Strips for Option 4	Pinwheel Sewn Unit
1-1/2	1	1	1-1/4	3/4	1-5/8	1-1/8	2	1-1/4	1
1-3/4	1-1/4	1-1/4	1-3/8	1	1-3/4	1-1/4	2-1/8	1-3/8	1-1/4
2	1-1/2	1-1/2	1-5/8	1-1/8	2	1-1/4	2-3/8	1-1/2	1-1/2
2-1/4	1-3/4	1-3/4	1-3/4	1-1/4	2-1/8	1-3/8	2-1/2	1-1/2	1-3/4
2-1/2	2	2	2	1-1/4	2-3/8	1-3/8	2-3/4	1-5/8	2
2-3/4	2-1/4	2-1/4	2-1/8	1-3/8	2-1/2	1-1/2	2-7/8	1-3/4	2-1/4
3	2-1/2	2-1/2	2-1/4	1-3/8	2-5/8	1-5/8	3	1-3/4	2-1/2
3-1/4	2-3/4	2-3/4	2-1/2	1-1/2	2-7/8	1-5/8	3-1/4	1-7/8	2-3/4
3-1/2	3	3	2-5/8	1-5/8	3	1-3/4	3-3/8	2	3
3-3/4	3-1/4	3-1/4	2-3/4	1-5/8	3-1/8	1-7/8	3-1/2	2	3-1/4
4	3-1/2	3-1/2	3	1-3/4	3-3/8	2	3-3/4	2-1/8	3-1/2
4-1/4	3-3/4	3-3/4	3-1/8	1-7/8	3-1/2	2	3-7/8	2-1/4	3-3/4
4-1/2	4	4	3-3/8	1-7/8	3-3/4	2-1/8	4-1/8	2-3/8	4
4-3/4	4-1/4	4-1/4	3-1/2	2	3-7/8	2-1/4	4-1/4	2-3/8	4-1/4
5	4-1/2	4-1/2	3-5/8	2-1/8	4	2-1/4	4-3/8	2-1/2	4-1/2
5-1/4	4-3/4	4-3/4	3-7/8	2-1/4	4-1/4	2-3/8	4-5/8	2-5/8	4-3/4
5-1/2	5	5	4	2-1/4	4-3/8	2-1/2	4-3/4	2-5/8	5
5-3/4	5-1/4	5-1/4	4-1/8	2-3/8	4-1/2	2-5/8	4-7/8	2-3/4	5-1/4
6	5-1/2	5-1/2	4-3/8	2-1/2	4-3/4	2-3/4	5-1/8	2-7/8	5-1/2
6-1/4	5-3/4	5-3/4	4-1/2	2-1/2	4-7/8	2-7/8	5-1/4	2-7/8	5-3/4
6-1/2	6	6	4-5/8	2-5/8	5	3	5-3/8	3	6

4 Patch Chart

A single square is used to create blocks.

				A Sewn or Graph Paper size Small Square	B Cut Size of Small Square	C Sewn or Graph Size of Block Square	D Cut Size of Block Square

A single square block diagram:
- A sewn size
- B cut size
- C block sewn size
- D block cut size

A Sewn or Graph Paper size Small Square	B Cut Size of Small Square	C Sewn or Graph Size of Block Square	D Cut Size of Block Square
1/2"	1"	1"	1-1/2"
3/4"	1-1/4"	1-1/2"	2"
1"	1-1/2"	2"	2-1/2"
1-1/4"	1-3/4"	2-1/2"	3"
1-1/2"	2"	3"	3-1/2"
1-3/4"	2-1/4"	3-1/2"	4"
2"	2-1/2"	4"	4-1/2"
2-1/4"	2-3/4"	4-1/2"	5"
2-1/2"	3"	5"	5-1/2"
2-3/4"	3-1/4"	5-1/2"	6"
3"	3-1/2"	6"	6-1/2"
3-1/4"	3-3/4"	6-1/2"	7"
3-1/2"	4"	7"	7-1/2"
3-3/4"	4-1/4"	7-1/2"	8"
4"	4-1/2"	8"	8-1/2"
4-1/4"	4-3/4"	8-1/2"	9"
4-1/2"	5"	9"	9-1/2"
4-3/4"	5-1/4"	9-1/2"	10"
5"	5-1/2"	10"	10-1/2"

9 Patch Chart

Block diagram:
- A sewn size
- B cut size
- C block sewn size
- D block cut size

A Sewn or Graph Paper size Small Square	B Cut Size of Small Square	C Sewn or Graph Size of Block Square	D Cut Size of Block Square
1/2"	1"	1-1/2"	2"
3/4"	1-1/4"	2-1/4"	2-3/4"
1"	1-1/2"	3"	3-1/2"
1-1/4"	1-3/4"	3-3/4"	4-1/4"
1-1/2"	2"	4-1/2"	5"
1-3/4"	2-1/4"	5-1/4"	5-3/4"
2"	2-1/2"	6"	6-1/2"
2-1/4"	2-3/4"	6-3/4"	7-1/4"
2-1/2"	3"	7-1/2"	8"
2-3/4"	3-1/4"	8-1/4"	8-3/4"
3"	3-1/2"	9"	9-1/2"
3-1/4"	3-3/4"	9-3/4"	10-1/4"
3-1/2"	4"	10-1/2"	11"
3-3/4"	4-1/4"	11-1/4"	11-3/4"
4"	4-1/2"	12"	12-1/2"

Setting Triangle Chart

Anytime you set a block on point, it will make the block look more intricate. Even a simple block can achieve more pizzazz by setting on the angle. When you choose to set a block on point it puts your quilt top on the diagonal. The quilt is sewn together in rows, on the diagonal. The rows are finished on each end with triangle units. Two opposite corners of the quilt top will need to have corner triangle units sewn to those two rows. The other 2 corner triangle units are sewn as a part of that diagonal row. Remember, we work with two measurements of a block: 1) Sewn-finished or graph paper size, and 2) cut or raw edge unit or block.

This chart will help you know the corner triangle unit and side setting triangle square units. If the size you require is not on the chart, then bump up to the next larger size. You will have room to trim it up perfect. And remember, all of us have our own private sewing and cutting measurements, even our sewing machines have their own private measurements!

Side Setting Triangle Units

Side triangles are created by cutting a square and then cutting it in half twice diagonally. This square will create 4 triangle units that will be the side triangle units.

Corner Setting Triangle Units

Corner triangles are required for each of the 4 corners of the quilt top. One square creates 2 triangle units. Each quilt top will require 2 squares for the 4 corners.

Sewn Finished or Graph Paper Size Block	Cut Square for Side Triangle Units	Cut Square for Corner Triangle Units
2"	4-1/8"	2-3/8"
3"	5-1/2"	3"
4"	7"	3-3/4"
5"	8-3/8"	4-1/2"
6"	9-3/4"	5-1/8"
7"	11-1/4"	5-7/8"
8"	12-5/8"	6-5/8"
9"	14"	7-1/4"
10"	15-1/2"	8"
12"	18-1/4"	9-3/8"

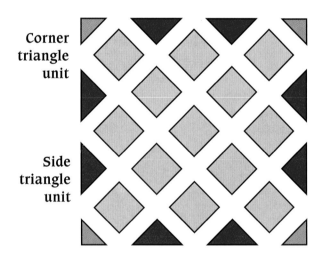

Corner triangle unit

Side triangle unit

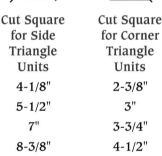

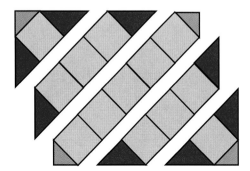

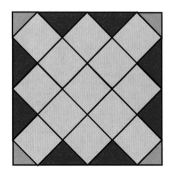

How to Square Up Your Quilt:

Lay your quilt on a smooth, flat area. Fold the short ends to the middle of the quilt. Do the edges all lay even? Is the middle the same size as the top and bottom? If it is not more than an inch, you have done well. Pat yourself on the back. If not, you need to ease or ooch some more. You may have to go deeper into the border to get it corrected. On the other hand, if it doesn't bother you, it doesn't bother me. Better luck next time.

How to Check for Square Corners on Your Quilt:

Lay your quilt out as described above. Do your corners have a true 90° edge when measured with a ruler? You may trim up to 1/4" without effecting your borders, more than that can cause odd border shapes and are noticeable to the eye. Borrow your husband's T square, if it helps, or use a ruler with the 45° line marked to help make miters.

All About Binding By Machine or Hand:

Binding is the finishing part. It makes a double layer around the edges of the quilt, keeping all 3 layers inside it. It can be done by machine or by hand. I cut most of mine 2-1/2" wide for large quilts and 2-1/4" for small. If machine binding (use a walking foot) is your choice, start on the back first. If by hand, start on the front. Follow pictures for "how to". Don't be afraid of those corners. They are not that hard.

Binding: Trim backing and batting even with the quilt

edge. Make sure corners are square. Use a ruler and a rotary cutter. You can check to see if your quilt is square by folding the ends to the middle. The edges should all be even with each other.

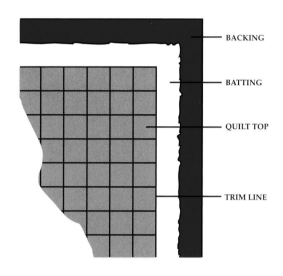

Straight of the grain binding is OK for most projects. If this is a big quilt, a contest or a Judged or Jury show quilt, use bias binding.

Trim ends at a 45° angle and sew binding in a long, continuous strip.

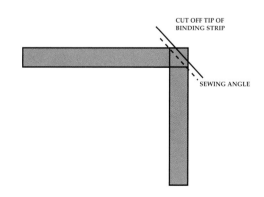

Step 1: Sew binding along edge of quilt, all edges even. Leave about 8" of binding loose at the starting point along the side of the quilt.

LEAVE ABOUT 8" LOOSE

SEW ABOUT 1/4" ALONG EDGE KEEPING ALL 5 EDGES EVEN

Step 2: Turn the binding at corner – stop 1/4" from bottom of quilt – backstitch – pull binding back up and pin. Lay binding back over bottom edge of quilt with a 45° mitered corner.

PIN TO HOLD 45° MITER

QUILT TOP AREA

BACKSTITCH 1/4" FROM EDGE

Step 3: Start stitching 1/4" from both sides of the corner. Be careful not to catch the full- ness of the mitered corner.

START SEWING 1/4" FROM TOP – SAME SPOT YOU QUIT SEWING AND BACKSTITCHED AT

Continue to sew around all 4 sides of quilt.

Step 4: To connect both ends, stop sewing about 10" from starting point – pin binding and quilt to center point and clip both binding strips.

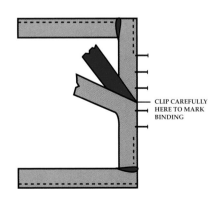

CLIP CAREFULLY HERE TO MARK BINDING

Step 5: Lay top binding over to the right – open it flat – face up. Bring bottom piece up – face down – connect clipped points and pin. Start sewing at left top corner of binding and sew down using a 45° angle to bottom right. Clipped points should line up evenly. Trim 1/4" from sewn line.

CUT 1/4" FROM SEAM

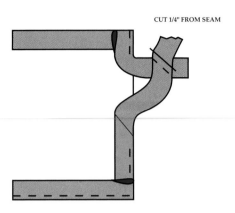

Step 6: After trimmed edges are off, it should lay flat against the quilt. Sew the binding down to quilt.

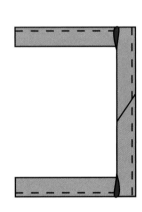

Step 7: Turn the binding over the edge of the quilt, keeping it smooth and tight. Blind stitch by hand or sew down using the sewing machine. If using the machine, attach the walking foot and slowly stitch down the binding very close to the edge. Use a stiletto and invisible thread.

Hint: remember the video shows the binding technique at the very end.

Christmas Star

32" x 32" • Beginner

This is the quilt for a quick and easy Christmas gift! You only need to make 4 green Option #14s and 2 in red. It's that easy, how simple can you get? You may substitute a solid square in the very center of the star or use the four squares as shown.

Fabric
8 different reds, fat quarters
8 different greens, fat quarter
1-1/4 yds. background muslin
4 2" x 27" strips red border = 1/4 yard
4 3" x 32" strips green border = 1/4 yard
1-1/2 yds. backing & binding fabric

Cutting
Cut 12 - 4-1/2" muslin squares for setting square (four make up the large center squares) *or*
Cut 1 - 8-1/2" center square and only 8 smaller squares
Cut 3 - 2-1/4" muslin strips for first round
Cut 6 - 3-3/4" muslin strips for 3rd round
Cut 4 - 4" green center squares
Cut 2 - 4" red center squares
Cut 1 - 2-5/8" of each red for second row
Cut 1 - 2-5/8" of each green for second row
Cut 4 - 2" red border
Cut 4 - 3" green border

Sewing
Refer to Option #14 for sewing and trimming instructions.

Step 1:
Start with two red 4" center squares. Sew 2-1/4" muslin strips to square. Trim up to the point of center square.

Step 2:
Sew 2nd row of 2-5/8" strips to your SnS®. Trim leaving 1/4" off of the tip of square.

Step 3:
Sew 3rd row of 3-3/4" muslin strips to your SnS®. Trim right up to the point or tip of the square.

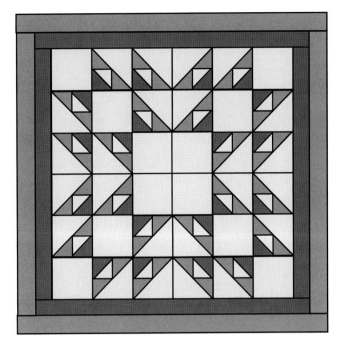

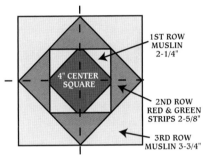

Step 4:
Cut in quarters as Option #14 shows. Repeat steps replacing red with green. Sewing 4 green, Option #14 SnS®.

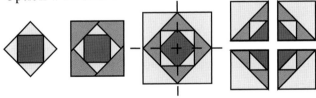

Step 5:
Sew muslin squares and Option #14 units in rows to create your Christmas Star. Pay careful attention to your red and green color placement. Outside star points are green. Inside start points are red. Sew a 2" red border to all 4 sides. Sew 3" green border to all 4 sides.

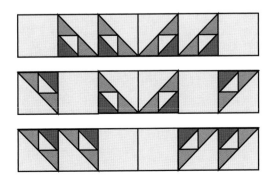

Shirttails

32" x 40" • Intermediate

Fabric

1 yd. each of 2 background colors - light
1/4 yd. light blue
1/4 yd. dark blue
3/8 yd. each black (3 blacks are used)
1/2 yd. red
binding included in black yardage
1 yd. backing fabric

Cutting

Cut 2 - 2-1/8" strips of all colors (each red, blue, black, and background)

Cut 1 - 2-1/8" strip into 20 - 2-1/8" red setting squares

OPTION 10

Cut 12 - 3-3/4" squares background lights (6 of each color)

Cut 2 - 2-1/4" strips of each blue and black (2 of each color)

Cut 8 - 2-3/4" of background color (4 of each color)

BORDER

Cut 4 - 1-1/4" strips of black for border

Cut 4 - 3" strips of red for border

Sewing

Step 1:
Sew 12 SnS® Option #10, 3-3/4" center squares, first row 2-1/4" blue or black, second row 2-3/4" background. (3 of each blue and 2 of each black.)

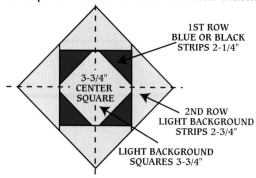

1ST ROW
BLUE OR BLACK
STRIPS 2-1/4"

3-3/4"
CENTER
SQUARE

2ND ROW
LIGHT BACKGROUND
STRIPS 2-3/4"

LIGHT BACKGROUND
SQUARES 3-3/4"

Step 2:
Sew 3 - 2-1/8" strips together of color-light-color and cross cut 2-1/8". You will need 12 - 3 patch units. 3 of each blue and 2 of each black. You may cut your strips in half on fold and sew short strips, the whole length is not needed for this size of quilt.

Step 3:
Sew a color 2-1/8" strip to each side of the 3 patch. (2-1/8" x 6" and size perfect for your block - 2-1/8" x 5-3/4").

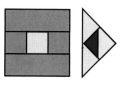

Step 4:
Sew Option #10 to each side, centering the Option #10 unit on the block sewn.

Step 5:
Sew sashing 2-1/8" background strips to 2 sides of 6 blocks. (2-1/8" x 8" and size perfect for your block - alternate background color of sashing strip.)

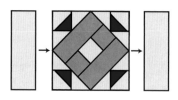

Step 6:
Sew 2-1/8" sashing strips to red 2-1/8" square, 5 squares, 4 sashings = sew 4 rows and sew quilt blocks to sashing strips. Size sashing strip length perfect for your block.

Step 7:
Sew black border and red border to all 4 sides of quilt. Refer to front of book for perfect border sizing.

Waves of Love

79" x 95" • Intermediate

Waves of Love is a beautiful quilt with thousands of triangles, and lots of piecing. Even with that in mind it is an easy quilt with only 2 blocks to master. This quilt uses Option #4 and Option #10. The Square in a Square® Technique will take the wavy worry out of this quilt and help you master with perfection the *try*-angle.

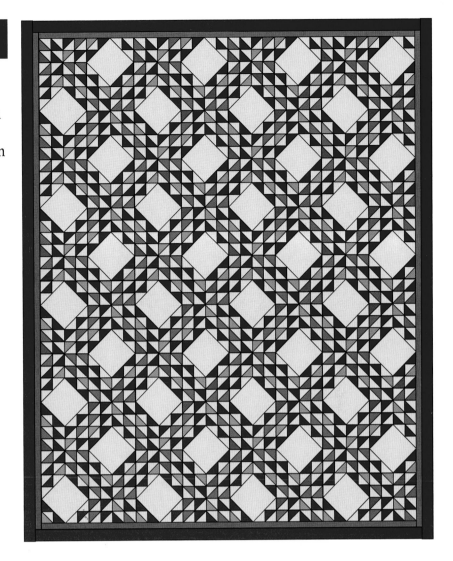

Fabric

6 yds. background fabric (Use a high quality of muslin or light print.)
9 shades of red totaling 7-1/2 yds. of fabric
3/4 yd. first border
1-1/2 yds. second border
1 yd. binding fabric
8 yds. backing fabric

Cutting

Cut 160 - 4" squares of muslin (Option #4 center - 16 strips)
Cut 6 - 2-1/4" strips of each shade of red for Option #4
Cut 40 - 6-1/8" squares of muslin - 7 strips
Cut 20 - 4" square of muslin - 2 strips for Option #10
Cut 20 - 4" squares of red print, use several colors
Cut 6 - 2-1/4" strips of muslin (Option #10)
Cut 9 - 2-1/4" strips, 1 of each red for Option #10
Cut 10 - 3" strips of muslin for Option #10
Cut 9 - 3" strips, 1 of each red for Option #10
Cut 8 - 2-1/2" strips for border 1
Cut 8 - 6" strips for border 2

Sewing

Step 1:
Sew 160 SnS® blocks, Option #4. Use a 4" muslin center square and 2-1/4" color strip. Use all shades of red. Estimated 6 strips of each shade of red.

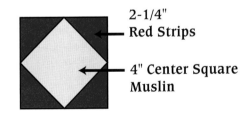

2-1/4"
Red Strips

4" **Center Square
Muslin**

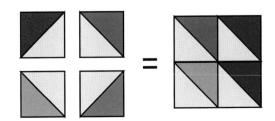

Step 2:

Sew Option #4 triangles in groups of 4. Sew your 4 triangle patches together. Sew 40 of this block. Sew 20 of these blocks with the color triangles going clockwise and 20 counter clockwise. Later, in Step 6, rows are sewn together in an alternating pattern to complete the design. Take it slow and watch as you go. Sewn 8", cut 8-1/2" block size.

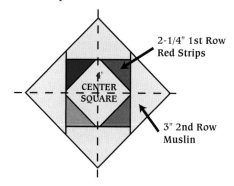

Step 3:

Sew 20 SnS® blocks, Option #10, creating triangle corners for your 6-1/8" muslin squares. Use 4" center muslin square, 2-1/4" strip first row red, 3" strip second row muslin.

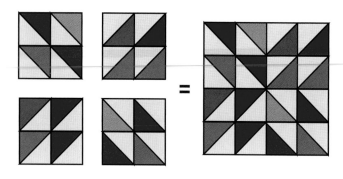

2-1/4" 1st Row
Red Strips

CENTER
SQUARE

3" 2nd Row
Muslin

Step 4:

Sew second set of 20 SnS® blocks, Option #10. Use 4" center red square, 2-1/4" strip first row muslin, 3" strip second row red.

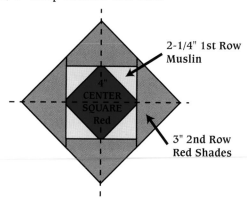

2-1/4" 1st Row
Muslin

4"
CENTER
SQUARE
Red

3" 2nd Row
Red Shades

Step 5:

Sew the Option #10 unit to your 6-1/8" muslin square. Alternate light and dark, Option #10, as you sew them to the 6-1/8" muslin square.

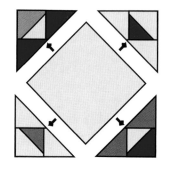 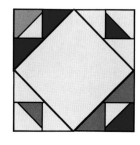

Step 6:

Alternate sewing the 2 blocks together in rows 8 across and 10 down. Carefully sew blocks together with the Step 5 block turning the same direction in that row. The next row is turned the opposite way. This will allow the light/dark triangle to match up. Sew border 1 on all 4 sides. Sew border 2 on all sides. Refer to the front of the book for border sewing information.

BLOCK SIZE
CUT 4-1/2" - SEWN 4"

	# of Strips to cut	Width of strip	Yield of units in strip	Block yields	Total Units		Estimated Fabric Amounts	
OPTION #10	1	2-5/8"	52	26	only 2 of the 4 are required for each block		26 blocks	1/8 yd.
Cut 2-5/8" square Cut 1-1/2" strip Cut 2" strip Cut 3-3/8" square	1	1-1/2"	12	6	strips required to surround the above center square for Option #10		12 blocks	1/8 yd.
	1	2	8	4	2nd row of strips to surround the Opt. #10		8 blocks	1/8 yd.
	1	3-3/8"	10	10	solid center		10 blocks	1/8 yd.
						Repeat in opposite light dark colors for the other 2 units.		
OPTION #4	1	2-5/8"	56	3	Center square for Option #4 - 4 options are required for each block for a total of 16 half square triangle units		3 blocks	1/8 yd.
Cut 2-5/8" square Cut 1-1/2" strip	3	1-1/2"	36	2	strips required to surround the above center square for Option #4		2 blocks	1/8 yd.
					16 half square triangles are required for each block. You will have leftover units.			

CUT 6-1/2" - SEWN 6"

	# of Strips to cut	Width of strip	Yield of units in strip	Block yields	Total Units		Estimated Fabric Amounts	
OPTION #10	1	3-3/8"	40	20	only 2 of the 4 are required for each block		20 blocks	1/8 yd.
Cut 3-3/8" square Cut 2" strip Cut 2-1/2" strip Cut 4-3/4" square	1	2"	8	4	strips required to surround the above center square for Option #10		8 blocks	1/8 yd.
	1	2-1/2"	8	4	2nd row of strips to surround the Opt. #10		12 blocks	1/4 yd.
	1	4-3/4"	8	8	solid center		16 blocks	1/3 yd.
						Repeat in opposite light dark colors for the other 2 units.		
OPTION #4	1	3-3/8"	44	2	Center square for Option #4 - 4 options are required for each block for a total of 16 half square triangle units		2 blocks	1/8 yd.
Cut 3-3/8" square Cut 2" strip	2	2"	16	1	strips required to surround the above center square for Option #4		2 blocks	1/8 yd.
					16 half square triangles are required for each block. You will have leftover units.			

CUT 8-1/2" - SEWN 8"

	# of Strips to cut	Width of strip	Yield of units in strip	Block yields	Total Units		Estimated Fabric Amounts	
OPTION #10	1	4"	40	20	only 2 of the 4 are required for each block		20 blocks	1/8 yd.
Cut 4" square Cut 2-1/4" strip Cut 3-1/4" strip Cut 6-1/4" square	1	2-1/4"	8	4	strips required to surround the above center square for Option #10		8 blocks	1/8 yd.
	1	3-1/4"	8	4	2nd row of strips to surround the Opt. #10		8 blocks	1/4 yd.
	1	6-1/4"	6	6	solid center		6 blocks	1/4 yd.
						Repeat in opposite light dark colors for the other 2 units.		
OPTION #4	1	4"	40	2	Center square for Option #4 - 4 options are required for each block for a total of 16 half square triangle units		4 blocks	1/4 yd.
Cut 4" square Cut 2-1/4" strip	2	2-1/4"	32	2	strips required to surround the above center square for Option #4		4 blocks	1/2 yd.
					16 half square triangles are required for each block. You will have leftover units.			

BLOCK SIZE
CUT 10-1/2" - SEWN 10"

OPTION #10

Cut 4-3/4" square
Cut 2-5/8" strip
Cut 3-5/8" strip
Cut 7-1/2" square

# of Strips to cut	Width of strip	Yield of units in strip	Block yields	Total Units	Estimated Fabric Amounts	
1	4-3/4"	32	16	only 2 of the 4 are required for each block	16 blocks	1/8 yd.
1	2-5/8"	8	4	strips required to surround the above center square for Option #10	8 blocks	1/8 yd.
1	3-5/8"	4	2	2nd row of strips to surround the Opt. #10	6 blocks	1/2 yd.
1	7-1/2"	5	5	solid center	5 blocks	1/4 yd.

Repeat in opposite light dark colors for the other 2 units.

OPTION #4

Cut 4-3/4" square
Cut 2-5/8" strip

# of Strips to cut	Width of strip	Yield of units in strip	Block yields	Total Units	Estimated Fabric Amounts	
1	4-3/4"	32	2	Center square for Option #4 - 4 options are required for each block for a total of 16 half square triangle units	6 blocks	1/3 yd.
4	2-5/8"	32	2	strips required to surround the above center square for Option #4	2 blocks	1/3 yd.

16 half square triangles are required for each block. You will have leftover units.

CUT 12-1/2" - SEWN 12"

OPTION #10

Cut 5-1/2" square
Cut 3" strip
Cut 4-1/4" strip
Cut 9" square

# of Strips to cut	Width of strip	Yield of units in strip	Block yields	Total Units	Estimated Fabric Amounts	
1	5-1/2"	28	14	only 2 of the 4 are required for each block	28 blocks	1/3 yd.
1	3"	8	4	strips required to surround the above center square for Option #10	8 blocks	1/4 yd.
1	4-1/4"	8	4	2nd row of strips to surround the Opt. #10	6 blocks	1/2 yd.
1	9"	9	9	solid center	9 blocks	1/8 yd.

Repeat in opposite light dark colors for the other 2 units.

OPTION #4

Cut 5-1/2" square
Cut 3" strip

# of Strips to cut	Width of strip	Yield of units in strip	Block yields	Total Units	Estimated Fabric Amounts	
1	5-1/2"	28	1	Center square for Option #4 - 4 options are required for each block for a total of 16 half square triangle units	2 blocks	1/3 yd.
2	3"	36	2	strips required to surround the above center square for Option #4	1 blocks	1/4 yd.

16 half square triangles are required for each block. You will have leftover units.

Ohio Star

36" x 40" • Beginner

A beginner can whip up this traditional scrap Ohio Star design so quick and easy. Option #3 and Option #1 are required with four solid squares. Review the block construction and the options to become prepared. Lets go!

Fabric
1/2 yard blue triangle setting
1/4 yard 6 squares cut 6 1/2" red check
3/4 yard background or light
4 strips selvedge to selvedge 1-1/2" red
    border 1
4 strips selvedge to selvedge 3-1/2" red print
    border 2
many scraps or strips 1-3/4" wide of reds-greens-blues-pinks-yellows-blacks-browns, at least 144 pieces 1-3/4" X 3-1/2" for Option #1 and #3, or 1 yd. total

Cutting & Sewing

Step 1:
Cut and sew 12 - 6" sewn Ohio Star blocks.

Option #3 - Flying Geese - Cut 24 center squares 3" background fabric and 1-3/4" strip of scraps to surround the 3" center square. Sew and trim basic square to the Option #3, Flying Geese.

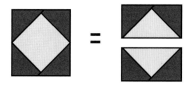

Option #1 - Square in a Square - cut 12 center squares 2-5/8" background fabric and 1-3/4" strip of scraps to surround the 2-5/8" center square. Sew and trim to an Option #1.

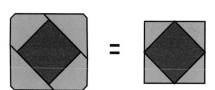

Step 2:
Sew Ohio Star together.

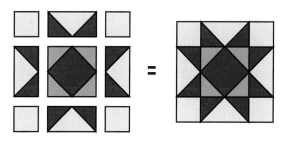

Step 3:
Cut 6 red check setting squares 6-1/2". Cut blue setting squares in triangle units and corner triangle units. Sew blocks into rows on the diagonal. These units are cut big so you can trim down for perfection.

2 - 6" squares into 2 corner units blue
3 - 10" squares into 4 side triangle units blue

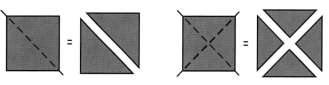

Step 4:
Cut and sew red border 1 - cut 1-1/2"
Cut and sew red border 2 - cut 3-1/2"

59

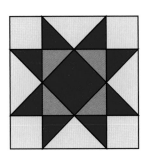 =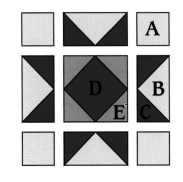

EACH STAR HAS:

4 corner squares (A)

4 star point units Option 3 (B,C)

1 center square Option 1 (D,E)

Multiply the number of star blocks you need by each number. Cut that amount.

BLOCK SIZE

CUT 3-1/2" - SEWN 3"

	# of Strips to cut	Width of strip		Block yield		Total units	Units leftover in strip	Estimated Fabric Amounts	
Cut 1-1/4" squares	1 -	1-1/4"	strip yields	8 blocks	=	32 squares	0	1/8 yd.	= 24 blocks
	1 -	2"	strip yields	10 blocks	=	20 squares	0	1/8 yd.	= 20 blocks
Cut 2" squares / Cut 1-1/4" strip	5 -	1-1/4"	strip yields	10 blocks	=	strips for the above 20 squares		1/2 yd.	= 20 blocks
Cut 1-5/8" squares / Cut 1-1/8" strip	1 -	1-5/8"	strip yields	22 blocks	=	center squares for Option 1		1/8 yd. =	44 blocks
	2 -	1-1/8"	strip yields	10 blocks	=	strips for above 22 squares		1/8 yd.	= 20 blocks

CUT 4-1/2" - SEWN 4"

	# of Strips to cut	Width of strip		Block yield		Total units	Units leftover in strip	Estimated Fabric Amounts	
Cut 1-1/2" squares	1 -	1-1/2"	strip yields	6 blocks	=	24 squares	2	1/8 yd.	= 12 blocks
	1 -	2-3/8"	strip yields	8 blocks	=	16 squares	1	1/4 yd.	= 24 blocks
Cut 2-3/8" squares / Cut 1-1/2" strip / Cut 2" squares / Cut 1-1/4" strip	4 -	1-1/2"	strip yields	8 blocks	=	strips for the above 16 squares		1/2 yd.	= 24 blocks
	1 -	2"	strip yields	20 blocks	=	center squares for Option 1		1/8 yd.	= 40 blocks
	3 -	1-1/4"	strip yields	16 blocks	=	strips for above 20 squares		1/4 yd.	= 16 blocks

CUT 5-1/2" - SEWN 5"

	# of Strips to cut	Width of strip		Block yield		Total units	Units leftover in strip	Estimated Fabric Amounts	
Cut 1-3/4" squares	1 -	1-3/4"	strip yields	4 blocks	=	16 squares	1	1/8 yd.	= 8 blocks
	1 -	2-5/8"	strip yields	7 blocks	=	14 squares	0	1/4 yd.	= 21 blocks
Cut 2-5/8" squares / Cut 1-5/8" strip / Cut 2-1/4" squares / Cut 1-3/8" strip	4 -	1-5/8"	strip yields	13 blocks	=	strips for the above 14 squares		1/4 yd.	= 13 blocks
	1 -	2-1/4"	strip yields	17 blocks	=	center squares for Option 1		1/8 yd.	= 17 blocks
	2 -	1-3/8"	strip yields	8 blocks	=	strips for above 17 squares		1/8 yd.	= 8 blocks

CUT 6-1/2" - SEWN 6"

	# of Strips to cut	Width of strip		Block yield		Total units	Units leftover in strip	Estimated Fabric Amounts	
Cut 2" squares	1 -	2"	strip yields	5 blocks	=	20 squares	0	1/8 yd.	= 5 blocks
	1 -	3"	strip yields	6 blocks	=	12 squares	1	1/4 yd.	= 18 blocks
Cut 3" squares / Cut 1-3/4" strip / Cut 2-5/8" squares / Cut 1-3/4" strip	4 -	1-3/4"	strip yields	6 blocks	=	strips for the above 12 squares		1/3 yd.	= 18 blocks
	1 -	2-5/8"	strip yields	14 blocks	=	center squares for Option 1		1/8 yd.	= 14 blocks
	4 -	1-3/4"	strip yields	19 blocks	=	strips for above 14 squares		1/3 yd.	= 12 blocks

BLOCK SIZE

CUT 7-1/2" - SEWN 7"

# of Strips to cut	Width of strip		Block yield		Total units	Units leftover in strip	Estimated Fabric Amounts	
1 -	2-1/4"	strip yields	4 blocks	=	16 squares	1	1/4 yd. =	12 blocks
1 -	3-3/8"	strip yields	5 blocks	=	10 squares	1	1/3 yd. =	15 blocks
2 -	2"	strip yields	6 blocks	=	strips for the above 10 squares		1/4 yd. =	12 blocks
1 -	3"	strip yields	13 blocks	=	center squares for Option 1		1/8 yd. =	13 blocks
4 -	1-3/4"	strip yields	13 blocks	=	strips for above 13 squares		1/4 yd. =	13 blocks

Cut 2-1/4" squares
Cut 3-3/8" squares
Cut 2" strip
Cut 3" squares
Cut 1-3/4" strip

CUT 8-1/2" - SEWN 8"

# of Strips to cut	Width of strip		Block yield		Total units	Units leftover in strip	Estimated Fabric Amounts	
1 -	2-1/2"	strip yields	4 blocks	=	16 squares	0	1/4 yd. =	12 blocks
1 -	3-3/4"	strip yields	5 blocks	=	10 squares	0	1/4 yd. =	10 blocks
5 -	2-1/8"	strip yields	5 blocks	=	strips for the above 10 squares		2/3 yd. =	10 blocks
1 -	3-3/8"	strip yields	10 blocks	=	center squares for Option 1		1/8 yd. =	10 blocks
3 -	1-7/8"	strip yields	10 blocks	=	strips for above 10 squares		1/4 yd. =	10 blocks

Cut 2-1/2" squares
Cut 3-3/4" squares
Cut 2-1/8" strip
Cut 3-3/8" squares
Cut 1-7/8" strip

CUT 9-1/2" - SEWN 9"

# of Strips to cut	Width of strip		Block yield		Total units	Units leftover in strip	Estimated Fabric Amounts	
1 -	2-3/4"	strip yields	3 blocks	=	12 squares	2	1/3 yd. =	9 blocks
1 -	4"	strip yields	5 blocks	=	10 squares	0	1/4 yd. =	10 blocks
5 -	2-1/4"	strip yields	5 blocks	=	strips for the above 10 squares		2/3 yd. =	10 blocks
1 -	3-5/8"	strip yields	10 blocks	=	center squares for Option 1		1/8 yd. =	10 blocks
3 -	2-1/8"	strip yields	10 blocks	=	strips for above 10 squares		1/4 yd. =	10 blocks

Cut 2-3/4" squares
Cut 4" squares
Cut 2-1/4" strip
Cut 3-5/8" squares
Cut 2-1/8" strip

CUT 10-1/2" - SEWN 10"

# of Strips to cut	Width of strip		Block yield		Total units	Units leftover in strip	Estimated Fabric Amounts	
1 -	3"	strip yields	3 blocks	=	12 squares	1	1/3 yd. =	9 blocks
1 -	4-3/8"	strip yields	4 blocks	=	8 squares	1	1/3 yd. =	8 blocks
5 -	2-1/2"	strip yields	5 blocks	=	strips for the above 8 squares		2/3 yd. =	10 blocks
1 -	4"	strip yields	10 blocks	=	center squares for Option 1		1/8 yd. =	10 blocks
3 -	2-1/4"	strip yields	10 blocks	=	strips for above 10 squares		1/4 yd. =	10 blocks

Cut 3" squares
Cut 4-3/8" squares
Cut 2-1/2" strip
Cut 4" squares
Cut 2-1/4" strip

CUT 11-1/2" - SEWN 11"

# of Strips to cut	Width of strip		Block yield		Total units	Units leftover in strip	Estimated Fabric Amounts	
1 -	3-1/4"	strip yields	3 blocks	=	12 squares	0	1/3 yd. =	9 blocks
1 -	4-7/8"	strip yields	4 blocks	=	8 squares	0	1/3 yd. =	12 blocks
4 -	2-5/8"	strip yields	4 blocks	=	strips for the above 8 squares		1/3 yd. =	12 blocks
1 -	4-1/2"	strip yields	8 blocks	=	center squares for Option 1		1/8 yd. =	8 blocks
2 -	2-1/2"	strip yields	8 blocks	=	strips for above 8 squares 1/3 yd. =			8 blocks

Cut 3-1/4" squares
Cut 4-7/8" squares
Cut 2-5/8" strip
Cut 4-1/2" squares
Cut 2-1/2" strip

CUT 12-1/2" - SEWN 12"

# of Strips to cut	Width of strip		Block yield		Total units	Units leftover in strip	Estimated Fabric Amounts	
1 -	3-1/2"	strip yields	2 blocks	=	8 squares	3	1/3 yd. =	6 blocks
1 -	5-1/8"	strip yields	4 blocks	=	8 squares	0	1/3 yd. =	8 blocks
4 -	2-7/8"	strip yields	4 blocks	=	strips for the above 8 squares		1/4 yd. =	8 blocks
1 -	4-3/4"	strip yields	8 blocks	=	center squares for Option 1		1/4 yd. =	8 blocks
2 -	2-3/4"	strip yields	4 blocks	=	strips for above 8 squares 1/2 yd. =			8 blocks

Cut 3-1/2" squares
Cut 5-1/8" squares
Cut 2-7/8" strip
Cut 4-3/4" squares
Cut 2-3/4" strip

Trip Around the Square

67" x 90" • Intermediate

This quilt is set together similar to the Trip Around the World. It uses Option #14. The Square in a Square® block yields 4 units. The quilt is 10 units x 14 units, which is 140 units or 35 SnS®. Simply use a light background or muslin with color scraps. I chose blues, golds, creams, and rust. Refer to Option #14 for SnS® instructions.

Fabric

4 yds. muslin
8 - 1/2 yd. pieces of medium color, small print, 4 yds. total
9 - 1/2 yd. pieces of dark color, small print, 4-1/2 yds. total
1-1/4 yd. dark blue border, cut 5-1/2" wide
3/4 yd. rust inside border cut 2-1/2" wide
1 yd. binding fabric
6 yds. backing fabric

Cutting

Cut 35 - 5" muslin center squares
Cut 10 - 2-3/4" color strips - first row*
Cut 20 - 3-5/8" muslin strips - second row*
Cut 24 - 4-3/4" color strips - third row*
Cut 8 - 2-1/2" strips for border 1
Cut 8 - 5-1/2" strips for outer border

*Number of strips required for Option #14 are an estimate. Your exact amount will vary.

Sewing

Step 1:
Sew 35 Option #14s. Refer to Option #14 and diagram above. Use color strips as scraps and alternate the usage of each color.

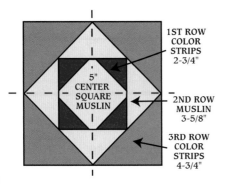

1ST ROW COLOR STRIPS 2-3/4"
5" CENTER SQUARE MUSLIN
2ND ROW MUSLIN 3-5/8"
3RD ROW COLOR STRIPS 4-3/4"

Step 2:
Sew the units together in any design you wish. This one starts in the center and the color goes out. My quilt is 67" x 90". When sewing your rows together, remember to put the large triangle up, then the large triangle down and continue to repeat. Sew in rows and then sew rows together. Divide quilt in rows, watch diagram above to receive placement help.

We Will Never Forget

69" x 80" • Beginner

This is a beginner quilt using Option #1 and a nine-patch. Red, white, and blue fabric with muslin shows off a traditional and quick quilt. Make this patriotic color scheme any size you wish! We worked on this quilt during our country's war on terrorism, in the Fall of 2001.

Fabric

2 fat quarters light print
6 fat quarters red
6 fat quarters navy
3 yards muslin or white
Border 1 - small border - 1-3/4 yard small blue
            print
Border 2 - wide border - 2 yards wide print
Border 3 - outside blue
            frame - 3/4 yard

Cutting & Sewing

To create our quilt, 20 blocks are required. Use 4 blocks across and 5 down. We also used Option #1 settings with sashing strips. Four additional blocks were sewn for corner border blocks. Refer to the front of book for nine-patch strip piecing

Step 1:
Cut and sew 24 Option #1s. Cut center square 2-5/8" using light print fabric - cut strips 1-3/4" (we rounded up) using red and navy. Option #1 cut size is 3-1/2".

Step 2:
Cut and sew 96 nine-patch units for 20 blocks and 4 borders blocks. Cut nine-patch strips of red, white (muslin) and blue 1-1/2". Raw edge size of nine-patch is 3-1/2".

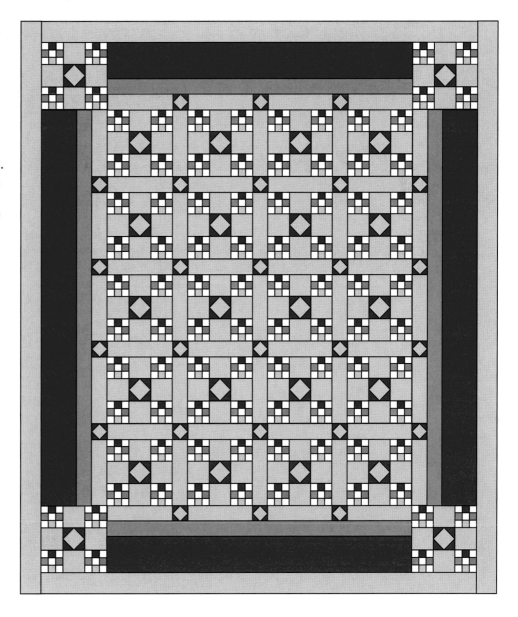

Step 3:

Cut 96 muslin or white squares 3-1/2". Sew above units into the large nine-patch block. 9-1/2" raw edge block.

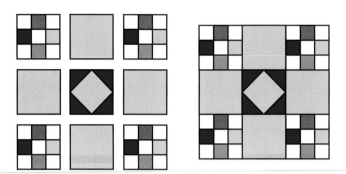

Step 4:

Cut and sew 26 Option #1 setting squares using a 2" center square of a light print and 1-1/4" red or blue strip. Raw edge Option #1 is 2-1/2". Cut 49 2-1/2" X 9-1/2" muslin sashing strips.

Step 5:

Sew blocks and sashing in rows. Sew as many rows as you need.

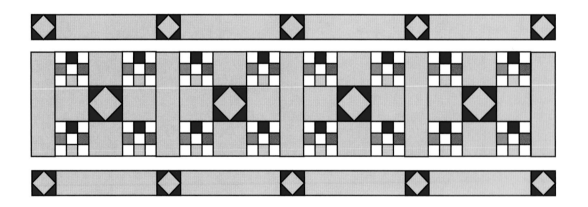

HINT: Leave the outside row of sashing and Option #1 setting squares off of the quilt. Sew the sashing and setting row as the first border.

Step 6:

Attaching the Border - remember to measure your quilt top for your accurate size. Cut and sew two sections. One top and one bottom. Cut two blue strips 2-1/2" x 42-1/2". Cut 2 print strips 7-1/2" x 44-1/2". Sew strips together and to quilt top and bottom. Repeat for sides using two blue strips 2-1/2" x 53-1/2", and two print strips 7-1/2" x 53-1/2". Attach corner blocks to this border section. Cut and sew 3" blue frame border, and sew on all four sides of quilt top. We used the same blue for the binding also.

Chinese Lantern

25" x 30" • Intermediate

Chinese Lanterns are made from the pineapple block using a triangle in the center of the block. Review the Option #12 - triangle pineapple block and you should be ready to go. Try doing a color variation where the lanterns would be stacked Jacko lanterns. It's all accomplished with the color placement. The strips in the quilt stay the same width each time you sew around the center. Make the quilt any size by changing the center unit size - strip width - and how many times you sew around the center unit.

Fabric

1/2 yd. light tan for center triangle and corner strips
1 fat quarter 1st row light lavender
1 fat quarter 2nd row light mint green
1/4 yd. 3rd row bubble gum pink and corner squares
1/3 yd. 4th row wedgewood blue
1/3 yd. 5th row medium green
1/2 yd. 6th row medium purple
1/4 yd. 1st border light pink
   2nd border included above in row 6
1/4 yd. binding
3/4 yd. backing

Cutting & Sewing

Step 1:
Cut 2" strips of tan - crosscut into 6 - equilateral triangles. Cut and sew 1-1/2" strips for all of the rows to sew around the center triangle. Refer to Option #12 triangle pineapple. Sew around your unit 6 rows in color order from above.

Step 2:
Cut and sew 2" and 3" corner strips to make the unit square. Square up the block.

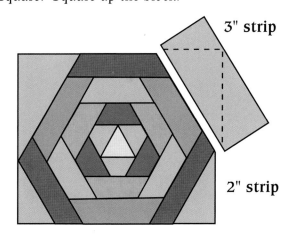

3" strip

2" strip

Step 3:
Cut and sew 1-1/2" border 1. Cut and sew 2-1/2" corner square and border strip.

Pineapple Picnic

45" x 55" • Beginner

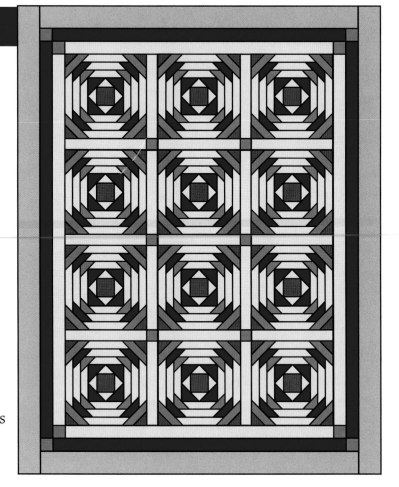

Fabric

1-1/4 yard blue flower print
1-1/4 yards white flower print
1 yard red flower print
3/4 yard blue check print
1 yard red check print
3/4 yard binding blue
3-1/2 yards backing print

Cutting

Cut 20 - 2" dark blue flower squares
Cut 28 - 1-1/2" white strips
Cut 16 - 1-1/2" red print strips
Cut 16 - 1-1/2" blue check strips
Cut 6 - 1-1/2" dark blue flower setting
　　　　　squares
Cut 6 - 2" dark blue flower print strips
Cut 17 - 1-1/2" x 9-1/2" white sashing strips
Cut 4 - 2" white strips - border 1
Cut 4 - 2" red strips - border 2
Cut 6 - 4-1/2" red check strips - border 3

Sewing

Step 1:
Review option #12 - Pineapple using a center square.

Sew 12 pineapple blocks using 2" blue center
　　square and 1-1/2" strips - 2" strips for row 9
Row 1 - 3 white strips
Row 2 - 3 red strips
Row 3 - 5 white strips - (when this row is
　　complete, the duplicate sides start to show)
Row 4 - 6 blue check strips
Row 5 - 7 white strips
Row 6 - 7 red strips
Row 7 - 8 white strips
Row 8 - 8 blue check strip
Row 9 - 6 - 2" dark blue strip

When you are ready to finish the block and make it square, add strips to all four corners of octagon unit and square the block up.

Step 2:
Sew pineapple blocks with sashing and setting units. Sew three blocks into a row. Repeat to complete the four rows.

Step 3:
Sew borders and corner setting squares. Sew top together to complete.

  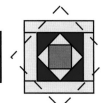 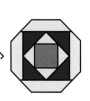 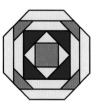 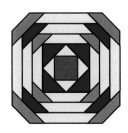 

Pineapple Diamond

39" x 42" • Intermediate

The pineapple block can be sewn with many different center units. The Square in a Square Ruler allows the square, triangle or diamond to be used in the center. This quilt uses the diamond. Refer to Options #7 for diamond strip cutting and Option #12 for overall pineapple trimming. This size of quilt with 9 diamond pineapple blocks and border can be sewn in about 8 or 9 hours. Have fun learning this option 12 and sewing the quilt!

Fabric

3/4 yard red
1/2 yard cream dot - 1st row and 5th row
3/4 yard dark green leaf - 2nd row and 8th row
3/4 yard light green leaf - 3rd row and 7th row
3/4 yard brown rose - 4th row and corner units
1/3 yard red vine for Border 1
1/2 yard brown with large rose for Border 2
1/2 yard for Binding
1-1/4 yard for Backing

Cutting & Sewing

Step 1:
Cut 1 red strip 2" crosscut into 9 diamonds. Refer to Option #7 diamond cutting.

Cut 3 cream dot strips - 1-1/2" - sew 1st row around diamond - trim. Refer to Option #7 and Option #12 trimming.

Step 2:
Cut 4 dark green strips - 1-1/2". Sew 2nd row around - trim 90 degree all 4 corners leaving seam allowance.

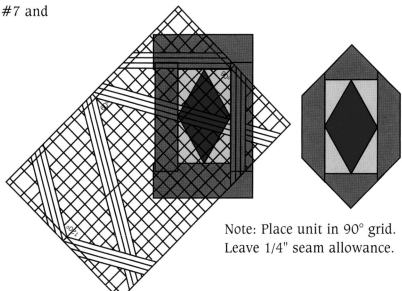

Note: Place unit in 90° grid. Leave 1/4" seam allowance.

Step 3:
Cut 4 light green strips - 1-1/2". Sew 3rd row around - two top and two bottom. Trim with 90 degree in tip leaving seam allowance. Trim sides even with previous strip edge and edge of ruler.

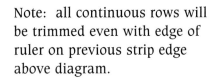

Step 4:
Cut 6 strips - 1-1/2" brown. Sew 4th row on all sides top-bottom-side-side and trim even with previous strip edge and edge of ruler. Continue to sew the strips in order of rows and required colors. Refer to fabric section of pattern.

Trim all with the edge of the ruler even with previous strip edge.

Note: all continuous rows will be trimmed even with edge of ruler on previous strip edge above diagram.

Step 5:
Cut 3 strips - 3-1/4" of brown for corner units for 4 blocks.

Cut 4 strips - 3-1/4" red for 5 blocks. Refer to diagram.

When you are ready to finish the block and make it square, add strips to all four corners of octagon unit and square the block up.

Step 6:
Cut 4 strips - 2-1/2" sew to quilt top with 4 - 2-1/2" green corner stones - Border 1.

Cut 4 strips - 3-1/2" sew to all sides of quilt top - Border 2.

In the Garden with Tumbling Blocks

48" x 55" • Intermediate

You would never believe that Option #1 is all that would be needed to create the Tumbling Block design! The most important part is the color and where you put it. A contrast that is clear, creates the easily seen depth in the block. All of the center squares of the options are the dark or black. A medium color value and a light color value were used for the strips sewn around the center squares of the options.

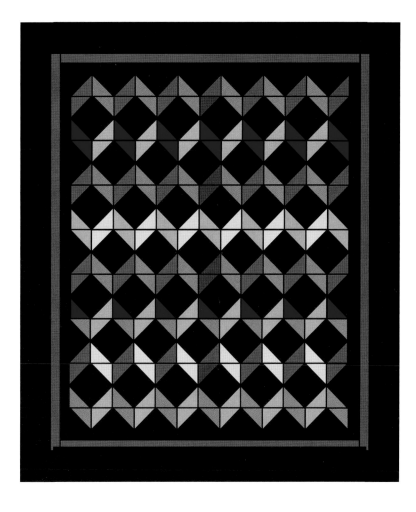

Fabric

1/2 yard - black (center units)

1/3 yard - of each color: orange, purple, green, blue and yellow.

1/4 yard - orange border

1-1/2 yards - black print borders

1 yard - binding black print

3 yards - backing black print

Cutting

Cut 1 - 3-3/4" black square

Cut 8 - 3-3/8" black squares

Cut 42 - 3" black squares

Cut several bright colors 1-3/4" (estimate a total of 40 strips - 5 strips each) orange, purple, green, blue, yellow

Cut 2 strips - 2" of each orange, purple, and green

Border 1 - cut 4 strips 3" black print

Border 2 - Cut 4 strips 2" vivid orange

Border 3 - Cut 4 strips 10" black print

Sewing

Step 1:
Sew three Option #3s, 3-3/8" black center squares with 2" strips each of purple and orange. Sew same color across from each other. Sew one Option #3 with orange and green. Sew four Option #3s with green and purple. The extra will be used for sides and bottom of quilt.

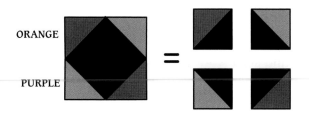

Step 2:
Sew one Option #4 - 3-3/4" black center square with 2" strips of orange and purple. Sew opposite color on each side as above.

Step 3:
Sew 42 Option #1s with 3" black center square and 1-3/4" strips in color combination required.

18 Option #1s	12 Option #1s	12 Option #1s
ORANGE — PURPLE / DARK BLUE — GREEN	ORANGE — PURPLE / GREEN — YELLOW	GREEN — PURPLE / YELLOW — ORANGE

Step 4:
Sew rows together watching color placement.

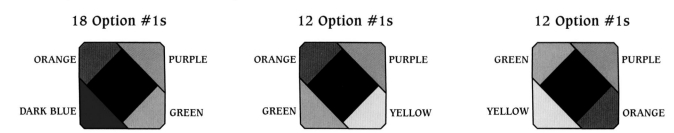

ROW 1 — PURPLE / ORANGE

ROW 2 — ORANGE PURPLE / DARK BLUE GREEN

ROW 3 — GREEN DARK BLUE / PURPLE ORANGE

ROW 4 — ORANGE PURPLE / GREEN YELLOW

ROW 5 — YELLOW GREEN / PURPLE ORANGE

ROW 6 — ORANGE PURPLE / DARK BLUE GREEN

ROW 7 — GREEN PURPLE / YELLOW ORANGE

ROW 8 — ORANGE YELLOW / PURPLE GREEN

ROW 9 — GREEN / PURPLE

Tumbling Block Chart

The tumbling block design has been commonly known as a difficult block. To do this handpiecing, templates and headaches were required. Now anyone can do it. Once again you will be amazed at how very easy it can be accomplished. The most difficult part will be your color or fabric placement. The sewing is only option#1! Now shut your mouth and start working on your color placement! If you don't want to mess with the color just divide your fabric into light- medium and dark. Have a clear definition of the color value. The medium will be the center square – the strips that are sewn around the center square will be dark - the light for the outside edges. When the rows are sewn together, they are stacked like bricks. Option 3 flying geese help complete the rows. Here is how you get started. Choose the option 1 size from the chart. Decide how many units across and down. Cut a few center squares. The bottom 2 strips or units will always be a darker shade of what the center unit is. The top 2 strips or units will be the areas you can play with. You can change and build or match up the option #1's.

Center squares are medium color strips or units on bottom are a darker shade of the center color.

Top triangles need to match up to the row above it – end units are light in color.

Watch how edges can be made to complete the box look.

For easy sewing and a neat look sew all options with opposite color on each side. Sew rows in the stack row formation; use an option #3 to complete the end.

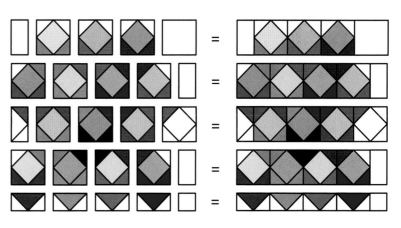

Option 1's Equal to Same Size Option 3			Option 3 Match up to Option 1 on the same row	
Sewn-Finished or Graph Paper Size	Cut Center Square	Cut Strip Size	Flying Goose Cut Center Square	Flying Goose Cut Strip Size
1	1-1/4	3/4	1-5/8	1-1/8
1-1/4	1-3/8	1	1-3/4	1-1/4
1-1/2	1-5/8	1-1/8	2	1-1/4
1-3/4	1-3/4	1-1/4	2-1/8	1-3/8
2	2	1-1/4	2-3/8	1-3/8
2-1/4	2-1/8	1-3/8	2-1/2	1-1/2
2-1/2	2-1/4	1-3/8	2-5/8	1-5/8
2-3/4	2-1/2	1-1/2	2-7/8	1-5/8
3	2-5/8	1-5/8	3	1-3/4
3-1/4	2-3/4	1-5/8	3-1/8	1-7/8
3-1/2	3	1-3/4	3-3/8	2
3-3/4	3-1/8	1-7/8	3-1/2	2
4	3-3/8	1-7/8	3-3/4	2-1/8
4-1/4	3-1/2	2	3-7/8	2-1/4
4-1/2	3-5/8	2-1/8	4	2-1/4
4-3/4	3-7/8	2-1/4	4-1/4	2-3/8
5	4	2-1/4	4-3/8	2-1/2

Moody Blues

34" x 41" • Intermediate

Four Option #4s create this Star unit. Cut and sew 4 options. You can use a variety of color strips on each side of the center square or keep the color strips consistent. This quilt uses the sewn 6" block - cut 6-1/2".

Fabric Requirements

3/4 yard - blue strips for star using many color values
3/4 yard - background for star - center square
2/3 yard - blue setting square and triangle setting units
1/4 yard - rust-red Border 1
1/2 yard - blue check Border 2
1/2 yard - binding fabric
1 yard   - backing fabric

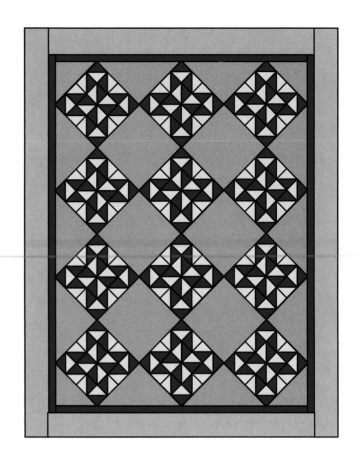

Cutting & Sewing

Step 1:
Cut and Sew 12 of the 6" sewn star blocks - using Option #4. Cut 3-3/8" background and 2" blue surround strips. Sew block together as below,

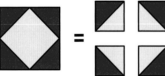

HINT: Remember that you will use more fabric of the strip amount.

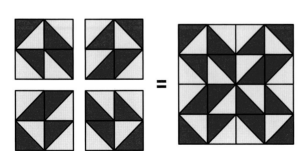

All 4 of these units are the same. Sew and turn for placement.

Step 2:
Cut 6 blue setting squares 6-1/2". Cut 2, 5-1/4" squares into 2 triangles each yielding 4 corner triangles. Cut 3, 9-3/4" squares into 4 side triangle settings. Units will yield 12 - you only need 10 - you will have 2 extra. Sew blocks into rows on the diagonal. Refer to pg. 50 for diagonal setting.

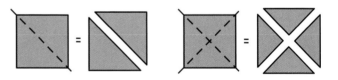

Step 3:
Cut and sew border 1 - 4 strips 1-1/2". Border 2 - 4 strips 4-1/2".

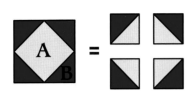 = 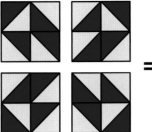 =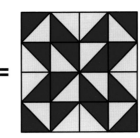

EACH STAR HAS:

16 half square triangle units which equals four Option #4s.

BLOCK SIZE
CUT 4-1/2" - SEWN 4"

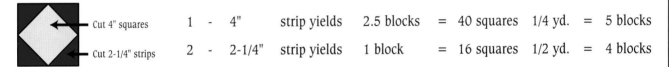

	# of Strips to cut	Width of strip		Block yield		Total units	Estimated Fabric Amounts		
Cut 2-5/8" squares	1 -	2-5/8"	strip yields	3.5 blocks	=	56 squares	1/4 yd.	=	10 blocks
Cut 1-1/2" strips	4 -	1-1/2"	strip yields	3 blocks	=	48 squares	1/3 yd.	=	6 blocks

CUT 6-1/2" - SEWN 6"

	# of Strips to cut	Width of strip		Block yield		Total units	Estimated Fabric Amounts		
Cut 3-3/8" squares	1 -	3-3/8"	strip yields	2.5 blocks	=	40 squares	1/4 yd.	=	5 blocks
Cut 2" strips	4 -	2"	strip yields	3 blocks	=	48 squares	1/4 yd.	=	6 blocks

CUT 8-1/2" - SEWN 8"

	# of Strips to cut	Width of strip		Block yield		Total units	Estimated Fabric Amounts		
Cut 4" squares	1 -	4"	strip yields	2.5 blocks	=	40 squares	1/4 yd.	=	5 blocks
Cut 2-1/4" strips	2 -	2-1/4"	strip yields	1 block	=	16 squares	1/2 yd.	=	4 blocks

CUT 10-1/2" - SEWN 10"

	# of Strips to cut	Width of strip		Block yield		Total units	Estimated Fabric Amounts		
Cut 4-3/4" squares	1 -	4-3/4"	strip yields	2 blocks	=	32 squares	1/3 yd.	=	6 blocks
Cut 2-5/8" strips	2 -	2-5/8"	strip yields	1 block	=	16 squares	1/3 yd.	=	2 blocks

CUT 12-1/2" - SEWN 12"

	# of Strips to cut	Width of strip		Block yield		Total units	Estimated Fabric Amounts		
Cut 5-1/2" squares	1 -	5-1/2"	strip yields	1.75 blocks	=	28 squares	1/2 yd.	=	5 blocks
Cut 3" strips	3 -	3"	strip yields	1 block	=	18 squares	1/4 yd.	=	1 block

Stars of Crimson

30" x 30" • Advanced

This beauty of a quilt is not hard! There is a lot of piecing, about 10 to 12 hours. It is a remarkable quilt to make and you will amaze yourself that you can do this. Option #1, #7 and #9 are required for this block. The challenge of this quilt is very easy using the Square in a Square® technique. Review Option #1, #7 and #9. The block size is a cut 6-1/2", sewn 6".

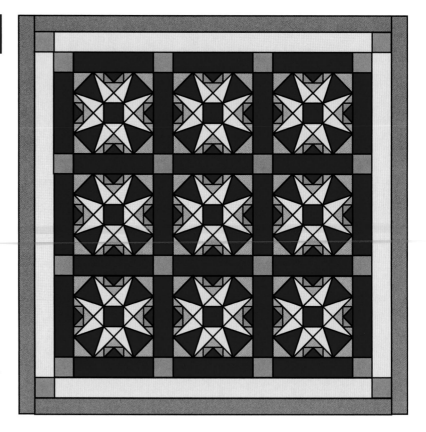

Fabric

1/2 yard - Star background light
1/2 yard - Red star points and corner stars
1 yard - Blue corners, setting square and
    outside border
1/4 yard - Medium tan, center of stars
1/4 yard - Multi black, Red sashing
1/4 yard - Light print inside border
1/2 yard - Binding
1 yard - Backing

Cutting

Label and group these together.

OPTION #1
Cut 1 strip 1-7/8" - red - cut into 9 - 1-7/8"
    squares
Cut 3 strips 1-1/4" - tan - surround strips for
    Option #1
:
OPTION #7
Cut 2 strips 2-1/2". Star background - cut into 18
    - diamonds 2-1/2", refer to Option #7
    diamond cutting.
Cut 6 strips 1-1/2" - red - star points

OPTION #9
Cut 1 strip 1-7/8" - background into 18 - 1-7/8"
    center squares
Cut 5 strips 1-1/4" - red - first row of surround
    strips of Option #9
Cut 5 strips 1-1/2" - background - 2nd row of
    surround strips of Option #9
Blue Corners - Cut 3 strips 2-1/4" - blue corner
    triangles on star points

SETTINGS SQUARES
Cut 1 strip 1-1/2" - blue - cut into 16 - 1-1/2"
    setting squares

SASHINGS
Cut 4 strips 1-1/2"- multi red-black - into 24 - 1-
    1/2" x 6-1/2" sashings

BORDER INSIDE
Cut 4 strips- 2"- light print
Cut 1 strip - 2" into red corner squares

BORDER OUTSIDE
Cut 4 strips - 3" blue border

Sewing

Step 1:
Option #1 - Sew 9 red 1-7/8" center squares with 1-1/4" tan strips into Option #1s and trim.

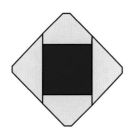

Step 4:
Sew blocks together. *(HINT: the Option #9 triangle unit will have a large dog ear, don't worry, it is your seam allowance.)* Sew 2-1/4" wide strips to corners and square the block up.

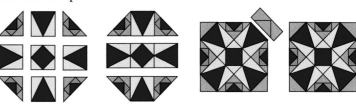

Step #2:
Option #7 - Sew 18 - 2-1/2" diamonds with 1-1/2" surround red strips star points into Option #7 and trim.

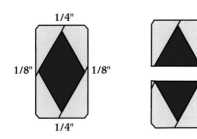

Step 5:
Sew sashing 1-1/2" x 6-1/2" and 1-1/2" setting squares in rows and sashing to stars in rows. Sew rows together. To complete quilt, sew borders and corner squares together and to the quilt top. Refer to border instructions in general directions.

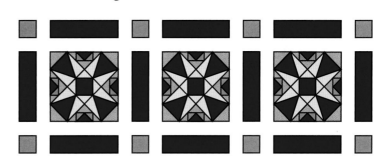

Step #3:
Option #9 - Sew 18 - 1-7/8" background squares with row #1 surround strips - red - 1-1/4" - trim as Option #9 shows. Sew row 2 surround strips background 1-1/2". Trim into Option #9 units.

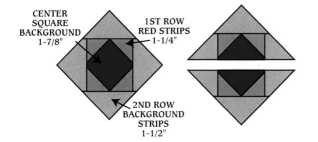

CENTER SQUARE BACKGROUND 1-7/8"
1ST ROW RED STRIPS 1-1/4"
2ND ROW BACKGROUND STRIPS 1-1/2"

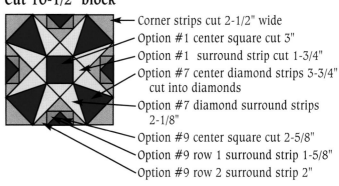

Sewn 10" block
Cut 10-1/2" block

- Corner strips cut 2-1/2" wide
- Option #1 center square cut 3"
- Option #1 surround strip cut 1-3/4"
- Option #7 center diamond strips 3-3/4" cut into diamonds
- Option #7 diamond surround strips 2-1/8"
- Option #9 center square cut 2-5/8"
- Option #9 row 1 surround strip 1-5/8"
- Option #9 row 2 surround strip 2"

Estimated fabric amounts for 10" sewn Star block

Option #1- center	39 - 3" squares in	1/4 yard	=	39 Star blocks
Option #1- strips	12 or 13 Options in	1/4 yard	=	12 Star blocks
Option #7- diamonds	16 Options in	1/4 yard	=	8 Star blocks
Option #7- strip	12 Options in	1/4 yard	=	6 Stars blocks
Option #9- center	42 Options in	1/4 yard	=	21 Star blocks
Option #9 - row 1	12 Options in	1/4 yard	=	6 Star blocks
Option #9 - row 2	12 Options in	1/4 yard	=	6 Star blocks
Corner unit	1-1/4 blocks in 1 strip	1/4 yard	=	9 blocks

Sassy Star

20" x 45" • Intermediate

Three Star Blocks are required for this adorable runner. Option #9 and #10 are required for the star plus 2 easy strip borders. Time requirements for the quilt top is 3 or 4 hours. Sewn block size is 12-1/2" x 12-1/2".

Fabric
1/2 yard - red- star points, Option #9 and setting triangle Option #10
3/4 yard - red green print - setting triangle Option #10 1st and 2nd row
1/2 yard - background light dot
1/4 yard - green dot center
1/4 yard - light strawberry
1/4 yard - border 1 dark green viney leaf
1/2 yard - border 2 green floral
1-1/2 yards backing & binding

Cutting
Option #9 Star:
Cut 1 - 4" strip into 6 - 4" squares using light dot fabric
Cut 3 - 2-1/4" strips red fabric - 1st row to surround the center Option #9
Cut 2 - 2-3/4" strips light dot row 2, Option #9
Cut 1 - 2-3/4" strip green dot row 2, Option #9
Cut 1 - 2-3/4" strip light strawberry row 2, Option #9

Option #10:
Cut 1 - 5-5/8" strip - red into 3 - 5-5/8" squares. Center of Option #10 will be corner triangle of the Star block
Cut 3 - 3" strips of red-green multi floral print for row 1 of Option #10
Cut 3 - 4-1/4" strips of red-green multi floral print for row 2 of Option #10

Border:
Cut 3 - 1-1/2" strips dark green for border 1
Cut 3 - 3" strips green floral large clear design for border 2

Sewing

Step 1

Option #9 Star:

Sew 4" center square with 2-1/4" surround strips for row 1. Watch this row of trimming (like Flying Geese Option #3). Two

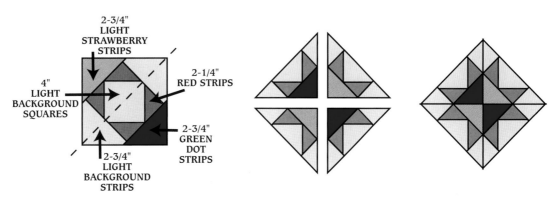

sides up to the point and other two sides leave 1/4" off of the center square point.

Sew 2 - 2-3/4" surround strips for row 2 using a light color dot. Sew one 2-3/4" surround strip for row 2 using the green dot. Sew one 2-3/4" surround strip for row 2 using light strawberry.

Step 2

Option #10:

Sew 3 SnS® blocks, refer to Option #10. Start with the 5-5/8" red center squares and 3" strips of the green multi print. Sew 2nd row of 4-1/4" green multi print. Remember to trim as you go referring to Option #10.

Sew units together and the 3 blocks to each other.

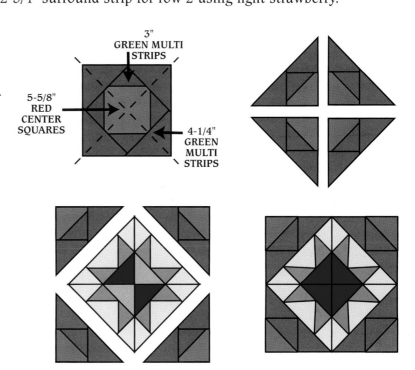

Step 3

Sew border 1 to all four sides and trim. Sew border 2 to all four sides and trim.

HINT: If you would like your table runner to have pointed or angled ends: Sew 1, Option #9 using the measurements as shown below for Option #9. The color placement will be a little different. Fabric yardage will not increase and you will have enough from the above amounts. When sewing the border, trim at the angles to "square up".

5-1/8" center square, green multi print • 2-3/4" row 1, red all four sides • 4" row 2, red all four sides

SEWN 4" - CUT 4-1/2"

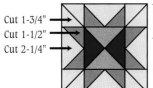

Cut 1-3/4" →
Cut 1-1/2" →
Cut 2-1/4" →

# of Strips to cut	Width of strip	Units in a strip	Block yield
1 -	1-3/4"	4	2
2 -	1-1/2"	6	3
1 -	2-1/4"	17	17

OPTION #10 corner units for star

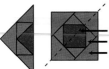

— Cut 3-1/8" center square
— Cut 1-3/4" strip for row 1
— Cut 2-1/2" strip for row 2

OPTION #9 for runner with angled ends

— Cut 2-7/8" center square
— Cut 1-3/4" strip for row 1
— Cut 2-1/4" strip for row 2

SEWN 7" - CUT 7-1/2"

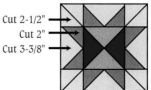

Cut 2-1/2" →
Cut 2" →
Cut 3-3/8" →

# of Strips to cut	Width of strip	Units in a strip	Block yield
3 -	2-1/2"	6	3
2 -	2"	6	3
1 -	3-3/8"	11	11

OPTION #10 corner units for star

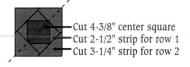

— Cut 4-3/4" center square
— Cut 2-5/8" strip for row 1
— Cut 3-5/8" strip for row 2

OPTION #9 for runner with angled ends

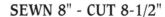

— Cut 4-3/8" center square
— Cut 2-1/2" strip for row 1
— Cut 3-1/4" strip for row 2

SEWN 5" - CUT 5-1/2"

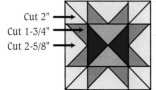

Cut 2" →
Cut 1-3/4" →
Cut 2-5/8" →

# of Strips to cut	Width of strip	Units in a strip	Block yield
2 -	2"	6	3
2 -	1-3/4"	6	3
1 -	2-5/8"	14	14

OPTION #10 corner units for star

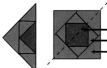

— Cut 3-5/8" center square
— Cut 2-1/8" strip for row 1
— Cut 3" strip for row 2

OPTION #9 for runner with angled ends

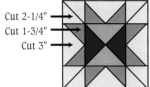

— Cut 3-3/8" center square
— Cut 2-1/8" strip for row 1
— Cut 2-1/2" strip for row 2

SEWN 8" - CUT 8-1/2"

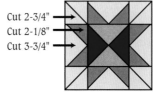

Cut 2-3/4" →
Cut 2-1/8" →
Cut 3-3/4" →

# of Strips to cut	Width of strip	Units in a strip	Block yield
2 -	2-3/4"	4	2
2 -	2-1/8"	4	2
1 -	3-3/4"	10	10

OPTION #10 corner units for star

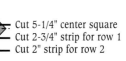

— Cut 5-1/4" center square
— Cut 2-3/4" strip for row 1
— Cut 2" strip for row 2

OPTION #9 for runner with angled ends

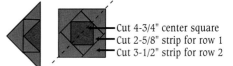

— Cut 4-3/4" center square
— Cut 2-5/8" strip for row 1
— Cut 3-1/2" strip for row 2

SEWN 6" - CUT 6-1/2"

Cut 2-1/4" →
Cut 1-3/4" →
Cut 3" →

# of Strips to cut	Width of strip	Units in a strip	Block yield
2 -	2-1/4"	6	3
2 -	1-3/4"	6	3
1 -	3"	13	13

OPTION #10 corner units for star

— Cut 4-1/4" center square
— Cut 2-3/8" strip for row 1
— Cut 3-3/8" strip for row 2

OPTION #9 for runner with angled ends

— Cut 3-7/8" center square
— Cut 2-1/4" strip for row 1
— Cut 3" strip for row 2

SEWN 9" - CUT 9-1/2"

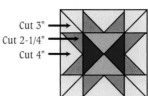

Cut 3" →
Cut 2-1/4" →
Cut 4" →

# of Strips to cut	Width of strip	Units in a strip	Block yield
2 -	3"	4	2
2 -	2-1/4"	4	2
1 -	4"	10	10

OPTION #10 corner units for star

— Cut 5-5/8" center square
— Cut 3" strip for row 1
— Cut 4-1/4" strip for row 2

OPTION #9 for runner with angled ends

— Cut 5-1/8" center square
— Cut 2-3/4" strip for row 1
— Cut 4" strip for row 2